COOKING
BACHELOR STYLE

TERRY L. MILLER

COOKING
BACHELOR STYLE
LIFE BEYOND THE FREEZER SECTION

TATE PUBLISHING & *Enterprises*

Cooking Bachelor Style
Copyright © 2010 by Terry L. Miller. All rights reserved.

No part of this publication may be reproduced, stored in a retrieval system or transmitted in any way by any means, electronic, mechanical, photocopy, recording or otherwise without the prior permission of the author except as provided by USA copyright law.

The opinions expressed by the author are not necessarily those of Tate Publishing, LLC.

Published by Tate Publishing & Enterprises, LLC
127 E. Trade Center Terrace | Mustang, Oklahoma 73064 USA
1.888.361.9473 | www.tatepublishing.com

Tate Publishing is committed to excellence in the publishing industry. The company reflects the philosophy established by the founders, based on Psalm 68:11,
"The Lord gave the word and great was the company of those who published it."

Book design copyright © 2010 by Tate Publishing, LLC. All rights reserved.
Cover design by Kandi Evans
Interior design by Stephanie Woloszyn

Published in the United States of America

ISBN: 978-1-61566-628-7
1. Cooking / Courses & Dishes / General
2. Humor / Topic / Adult
10.01.06

DEDICATION

To God, for it is through him that I have the ability to write. My talent is on loan from him. I'm thankful for it every day.

To my mother, who has triumphed over adversity and still managed to live a good life, always having time for her kids. And although I know she may have wondered at times which road I would travel, she never lost faith.

And to my father, although he is no longer with us, he remains a powerful influence in my life. His rise from a grade-school dropout to a respected figure in the corporate world has been a strength for me for as long as I can remember. I miss him dearly, but for this book, I know he would be proud.

TABLE OF CONTENTS

Foreword 11
Introduction 13
Kitchen Help 15

Breakfast

What Do Women Want? 19
Grasshoppers, Puss Puss, and Elma 22
The Million-Dollar Sandwich 24
What in Sam Hill Is That? 26
Frita and Her Toast Are Not French 29
Of Sake, Women, and Leftover Noodles 30
A Roman Berry Picking 32
Mushroom Cloud 34
Can the Ham 36
Lost in Translation 38

Lunch

A Fish Tale 41
Barefoot and Single in the Kitchen, ... 43
    a Recipe for Bologna Barbecue
Sour Note 45
A Foxy UFO 47
Courting a Lounge Lizard 50
The Birds, the Bees, and Maggie 52
The Tennessee Two-Step 54
Where's the Beef? 56

"Down in Louisiana Where the Black Trees Grow" 59
In a Pickle over Lunch... 61
From Russia with Love... 63
The Ugly Side of Grapes 65
Valentine's Showdown 68
Say Cheese!... 71
Out of Africa 73
Bigfoot Blasphemy 76

Dinner

Love Ain't a Walk in the Park 79
Boared to Death 81
Three Piggy Pork Sandwich... 83
East Meats West... 84
It's Miller Time 87
Shotgun, Shells, and Sausage.. 89
Cabbage Patch Cooking 91
Baby Blues 92
Race to the Finish 95
Calling Dr. Love.. 97
Ninja Chicken... 100
Terry Had a Little Lamb (and Mother Cooked It)............... 103
Playing Opossum—Deplorable Ploy.................................... 105
The Garden of Good and Spooky 108
Love in a Bucket 110
"Tanked" Giving, Pilgrim Style.. 113
What Sex on the Beach?.. 115
Out of Ashes, a New Bird 118
Fried Fish, Better Than a Stick in the Eye 120
Outdated Date... 122
The Santa Claus Shuffle.. 124
Real Men, Where Are You? 127
Pasta Overload.. 129

Appetizers

Over the Ocean Blue...or Black.. 133
Philosophy 101 Minus Eleven 135
Hold the Bacon, Please! 139
The Cereal Lady Killer 141
Clean Slate 143
Suckered in Seoul... 146
Jailhouse Jezebel.. 148
One Potato, Two Potato.. 151
Himalayan Nachos (Bachelor Style).. 151

Index 155

FOREWORD

What does a hapless, lonely bachelor do in between hilarious failed attempts at relationships?

He eats.

To do that, he has to cook. Since most of his energies are directed at seeking out women, the recipes have to be simple. So Terry Miller creates recipes—for breakfast, lunch, dinner. They're quick, easy, and should be in every kitchen, whether you're a bachelor or a woman who wants her mate to occasionally cook.

But let's not overemphasize food.

Terry's adventures preceding each recipe are the essence of *Cooking Bachelor Style.* He travels from Louisiana to Pennsylvania to Idaho and California in search of work and women, mainly women. Who else could combine elements of stolen gas, a burning cigar, and an ill-timed case of flatulence that sets off a chain of fire events ending on his butt? Who else watches helplessly as a romantic picnic turns bad with the entrance of the seagulls from hell?

Nearly everyone can relate to a person looking for a mate but just not being able to commit to a long-term relationship. Sometimes the end comes through a series of extremely embarrassing blunders, and sometimes it's just the difference between the way a man and a woman see the same thing.

The situations will make you shake your head, cringe, and laugh out loud. *Cooking Bachelor Style* is probably the funniest book you'll read all year.

The beauty of *Cooking Bachelor Style* is that when you're finished sharing a Terry adventure, you can go to the recipe and share a bite to eat.

—Harry J. Beird, retired humorist

INTRODUCTION

Are you a male between the ages of eighteen and seventy-five eating frozen waffles for breakfast, frozen potpies for lunch, and TV dinners for supper?

Have you never held an interest in cooking because following instructions in a traditional cookbook is more like trying to complete a scientifically measured experiment?

I still don't know where recipe makers in traditional cookbooks get their precise measurements. I do know, however, that combining those half-teaspoons of this and quarter-tablespoons of that can be a tedious task.

And that's why I'm here.

I have lived the bachelor's life since conception. Yes, I've done the frozen waffles, potpies, and TV dinners. And when that became so boring I couldn't stand it, I even tried to navigate through the instructions in a traditional cookbook. I not only cooked myself into frustration, I wound up with a cupboard full of spices and ingredients that still sit there gathering dust.

That's when I began preparing my own dishes and those from fellow bachelors. Simple stuff. Different combinations of things on hand. No rosemary, thyme, tarragon leaves, parsley, or poppy seeds. Nothing fancy, all fun. And speaking of fun, if you've ever been ambushed by the opposite sex, I think you'll enjoy the stories that accompany each recipe. Bachelorhood can take you on the ride of a lifetime, and it does in *Cooking Bachelor Style*. See why one woman will probably never go on a picnic again after being beaten up by birds. Or what happens when body language is misread during a date. You'll even read what happens when the author ingests the wrong kind of mushroom in a New Mexico desert.

Cooking Bachelor Style will deliver a smile to your face and a meal to boot.

You don't have to be a chef or a food scientist to prepare these recipes. They're quick, cheap, and easy. I can't tell you the measurements of saturated fats, carbohydrates, sodium, protein, sugars, fibers, or cholesterol in these dishes. But if you would like to cook at home without hassle and spending a lot for spices and items you'll never cook with again, this is a book you'll appreciate.

Come on out of the freezer. You too can be *Cooking Bachelor Style*.

KITCHEN HELP

Before you begin to sharpen your cooking skills, here is a list of items that anyone living alone, or who has never cooked, should have. Take stock of these items and you'll be fine.

- **Spices**: salt, pepper, garlic, garlic salt, bouillon cubes (chicken, beef, vegetable), chicken seasoning, and chili powder
- **Packets of gravy mixes**: chicken, brown, white, and pork
- **Canned "cream of" soups:** mushroom, celery, clam chowder, chicken, broccoli, and potato
- **Canned broths**: chicken and beef
- **Canned meats**: chicken, clams, and tuna
- **Canned tomatoes**: whole tomatoes, tomato paste, tomato sauce, diced tomatoes, stewed tomatoes, and spaghetti sauce

- **Canned vegetables**: corn, peas, mushrooms, mixed vegetables, and carrots
- **Canned beans**: kidney beans, green beans, pork and beans, pinto beans, baked beans, lima beans, and chili beans
- **Things not to be without**: pasta (spaghetti, rings, egg noodles, virtually any shape and size), flour, corn starch, baking soda, brown sugar, baking powder, and white or brown rice

Temperatures for the Oven

While we're here, let's set the oven temperatures to help when a dish calls for baking:

- **Warm:** 250–275 degrees
- **Low:** 300–325 degrees
- **Medium:** 350–375 degrees
- **High:** 400–425 degrees
- **Very High:** 450–475 degrees

Utensils You'll Find Handy for the Kitchen

1. A nice set of measuring cups. These are individual cups and come in the following measuring amounts: ¼, ⅓, ½, ⅔, ¾, and 1 cup.
2. A one-quart container and a one-pint container for measuring water. Handy when making soups.
3. A good wooden spoon.
4. Two to three different sizes of nonstick frying pans and saucepans.

KITCHEN HELP

5. A nice Crock-Pot will also come in handy.
6. A five-quart cooking pot.
7. A couple nice casserole dishes.
8. Several different sizes of plastic bowls with lids for storing leftovers.
9. A colander for draining water off spaghetti and vegetables. This is one of those containers with 980 holes in it.
10. A sharp knife for cutting veggies, and a steak knife for cutting meats.
11. A cookie sheet (for broiling, not cookies)!
12. A good can opener will be your best friend.
13. A turkey baster will also come in handy when doing chickens, or even the "big bird" when you're having a party. This is one of those gadgets that you put in liquid, squeeze and release the end of it, and it draws liquid into it. You squeeze it again and it releases it. Yeah, you know the thing I'm talking about. You won't use it a whole lot, but it's a useful tool.
14. A good, sturdy pancake turner.
15. A potato masher (handy for making egg salad too).
16. A whisk, or fork, for mixing.
17. Large and small freezer bags for freezing leftovers.

This may look like a lot of stuff, but it's really not. Compared to some kitchens where different dishes and utensils take up space and rarely get used, these are the bare essentials that will carry you a long way. Happy cooking!

BREAKFAST

What Do Women Want?

For centuries, men have been plagued by the question, "What do women want in a relationship?" It's a question that's driven men to drink, divorce, grow gray hair, lose hair, and become so utterly frustrated that they seek professional help.

But even the professionals are hard-pressed to answer such a perplexing question.

Women pose a very unique challenge to men. It's been that way throughout history, and it is destined to remain that way until the world no longer turns. It's as if when God took Adam's rib to create Eve, he also took the part of Adam's brain that could logically deduce what would please her for the rest of her life. And it's evident Adam couldn't please her; hence, the pre-menstrual-cramp-induced-apple-biting episode.

If one of the most perfect creatures on earth (Adam) couldn't keep a happy relationship, what chance do you and I stand? It's a valid question and a good one.

When you ask most men, "What do women want in a relationship?" one is hard-pressed to get an answer. Ninety-nine out of one hundred times men will throw their hands in the air and say nothing. And ninety-seven out of one hundred times what they think makes a woman happy today isn't the same thing that will make a woman happy tomorrow.

What I've attempted to do in the following summation is to give men a little deeper insight into what women are looking for in order to form and maintain a happy partnership. I've never studied doctoral information nor performed any psychiatric evaluations. I'm just a man who set out to find answers to one of the most baffling questions ever asked.

What I'm about to share with you can change your life and help you see women in a whole new light. That light may not always shine, but you'll have a better understanding of the woman beside you, or the one for whom you are searching.

My journey into the female psyche was unique, compelling, and satisfying. I've talked with many women and have had to submit myself to some pretty unorthodox situations. But it was for the benefit of all of us who call ourselves bachelors. If women have you on the edge of a cliff ready to take the dive, heed the following. You'll have a whole new perspective on the opposite sex.

First and foremost, don't try to figure the woman out. There is no equation. Two plus two does not equal four. The hand that feeds will get bit. Blue is not blue, yellow is not yellow, pink is not pink.

Secondly, the answers to your questions today may not be the answers to your questions tomorrow. If today she says that tomorrow she wants tacos for dinner, check again tomorrow. Because in that lost land we call sleep, pixies do play. They'll take your conversations from the daylight hours and in the dead of night, wearing their mischievous little grins, rearrange words, sentences, and entire phrases in the woman's head. And when she awakes in the morning, the results of the pixie playground will leave you scratching your head. What made sense yesterday is confusion today. Always check twice.

Finally, learn to think smart. Never, ever, *ever* violate her vanity. If she asks if the jeans she's wearing make her look fat, the answer is always a resounding no! If she asks, "Do I look sexy?" the answer is emphatically yes! *Yes* and *no* are two of the smallest words in the dictionary, but they are two of the biggest causes of calamity for men involving women. They are tricky little words that can easily be used incorrectly when answering your mate, girlfriend, or overnight guest.

I can't reiterate enough: think smart.

This diminutive summation will help immensely when dealing with this delicate entity we call woman. But remember, one tip is no less important than the others.

Although these words of advice will help you tremendously in the sea of femininity, there are two more words that apply equally as well:

Good luck.

In the meantime, you can enjoy this no-brainer of a breakfast.

Egg and Veggie Scramble

- Serves 2
- Prep time—about 5 minutes
- Cook time—about 15 minutes

6 eggs

4 strips of cooked bacon

1 cup of succotash (15 oz., drained)
   (Succotash is lima beans and corn. If you don't care for limas, just use a can of kernel corn.)

Milk

In a medium-sized nonstick frying pan, cook bacon until crisp. Drain fat; break into pieces and return to pan. In a mixing bowl, mix eggs and a splash of milk (remember a splash is tipping the container for about a second) and stir until yolks are broken. Add the succotash, stir again, and pour over bacon bits. Stir once again to mix in bacon and cook over medium heat, stirring occasionally until eggs are done. Good stuff!

Grasshoppers, Puss Puss, and Elma

I once lived with a woman who thought she could capture the world through her cooking. Her heart was in the right place, but…

I remember waking up one morning to the high-pitched scream of a blender. It was a horrible sound at five forty-five in the morning. The shrill whirl was a rude awakening, much worse than an alarm clock. With an alarm clock you at least have the option of shutting the darn thing off. That blasted blender must have run for twenty minutes, maybe more. Meanwhile, I could hear Elma singing the lyrics to "Happiest Girl in the Whole USA." For those of you under forty who don't know, that song was the ultimate female "feel good" tune some years ago.

When the blender stopped, along with the fifth rendition of that song, I was summoned downstairs to breakfast. (I use the term *breakfast* loosely.) As I slowly made my way down the stairs, my stomach began a steady counterclockwise turn. It was a signal I had learned to respect when it came to Elma's cooking. And my stomach was once again right on cue. As I ambled into the kitchen, there before me, as grand as a mother sow suckling her tiny pigs, stood a large glass of a concoction consisting of a green, frothy liquid. The fluid looked like two hundred grasshoppers, with a hint of dirt, blended to perfection. If you've never seen two hundred grasshoppers, with a hint of dirt, blended to perfection, the color is a cross between pea soup and ham gravy. It looked beyond disgusting.

But probably worse than the color was the way it smelled. The odor was somewhere between stale beer and cat pee. I can't tell you what she had mixed or how it tasted because as Elma proudly carried her "breakfast" to the bathroom to sip as she built her day face, I poured mine into the cat dish.

That turned out to be a deadly mistake.

Puss Puss, a yellow-haired stray I had taken in, lapped hungrily at the off-colored cocktail. I couldn't understand why she lapped so furiously at the strange mixture. It was only after the cat finished eating and began cleaning her whiskers and paws that I noticed a peculiar look in her tiny green eyes. Puss Puss sat squarely on the floor and alternately looked at me and the empty dish, her head circling in a dizzying motion. I immediately felt bad for feeding the strange brew to her and knew no good was going to come of it. And I was right. The cat's entire body began to balloon, starting in her face. I opened the sliding glass door and tossed her into the grass, fearful she might detonate.

I never saw poor Puss Puss again. My fear of her exploding, however, was realized two weeks later when I noticed tiny strands of cat hair hanging from the pussy willow tree in the backyard.

That discovery was the end of both Puss Puss and Elma. It wasn't hard getting over Elma, but to this day, each time I pass the pussy willows, I think of poor Puss Puss and pout.

And to this day, I hold great disdain for grasshoppers.

The end to Puss Puss and Elma was not without its merits, however. It helped me discover breakfast on my own. The following is one of many creations that came from their demise. I guarantee it will taste better than a grasshopper shake.

Mexican Omelet

- Serves 1
- Prep time—about 5 minutes
- Cook time—about 20 minutes

3 eggs

Milk

Butter

2 American or cheddar processed cheese slices

Salsa from a jar

Garlic powder

Preheat a medium to large frying pan over low heat. Melt 1 tablespoon of butter slowly. As the butter is melting, in a mixing bowl crack the three eggs and add a splash of milk. Now, a splash of milk is not pouring it in; it's not adding a drop. A splash of milk is taking your carton and tipping it for about 1 second. That's a splash. Once your milk is added, take your garlic powder and add about 2 to 3 good shakes. With a whisk or fork, mix everything until well blended. In other words, you'll have one uniform color.

By now your butter should be melted. Add eggs to the pan. Turn up your heat just a tad and cook the eggs until they are nearly set. This will take a few minutes. Don't get impatient and crank up the heat, or you'll burn them. To help the process along, once the eggs begin to set, take a pancake turner and lift one of the edges of the egg and tilt the pan so the runny egg on top runs to the opening you've left. Do this all the way around the pan so it drains evenly.

When the omelet is almost set (you can tell when there is very little loose egg left), imagine cutting the whole thing in half and spoon out about 3 tablespoons of salsa, making a line down one half of the eggs. Rip your cheese slices in half and lay them over the same half of the eggs, covering the salsa.

Now the tricky part. With your pancake turner, very carefully fold the egg in half so that the half without the filling covers the half with the filling. This might take some practice, but it's quite easy once you get the hang of it.

When you have the egg folded, cover and turn off your heat and let the omelet set for about 7 to 8 minutes to allow the salsa to heat through and cheese to melt.

The Million-Dollar Sandwich

Have you ever had an idea that would have made you a millionaire had you only known how well the public would have responded to it? I have. This muffin sandwich was born of poverty, but it has become one of the biggest-selling breakfast sandwiches in the world. After reading this, you'll know what I'm talking about.

BREAKFAST

I was living in New Mexico at the time this recipe was born on a diet of cactus soup and rattlesnake steaks. Now, that diet may sound like some cowboy tale from the 1880s where some old haggard soul is living in the desert after Indians raided his ranch and burned it to the ground. But it's not. This was in 1973, and I was living in the wasteland after my buddy, Sam Little Cloud, got drunk and drove my riding mower into the side of my house, causing a huge explosion when his cigarette rolled into the stream of gas leaking from the busted gas tank.

It may seem strange having a riding mower in the desert, but it was the closest thing to a four-wheeler I could afford.

In an old Navaho cave, I lived on cactus needle soup and rattlesnake steaks for nearly four months before a band of wandering gypsies drifted by and welcomed me into their group. The gypsies had with them four pigs, eighteen chickens, and a whole bunch of rum. We ate well as we traversed the desert. They shared their eggs and I shared my soup and steak recipes. At night, we drank rum and swapped stories around a tumbleweed fire as the band's fiddler played in the background.

Late one night, we settled in for the evening on the outskirts of a small town in southern New Mexico. Around midnight, one of the gypsy women came back from town carrying a small package of English muffins and a big chunk of cheese wrapped in burlap. She said she had traded a chicken for the fare. But evidently, no one had ever eaten an English muffin because no one knew what to do with them. I was born with a knack for coming up with recipes with things on hand, and I was rummed up enough to make a suggestion.

We left camp the next day with one less pig, one less chicken, nine pounding headaches, and a bunch of full bellies. My muffin sandwich was a huge hit.

If you go to one of those express joints and eat one of their muffin sandwiches, remember it originated in the deserts of New Mexico with a pig, a chicken, a bag of muffins, a chunk of cheese wrapped in burlap, and a band of nomads.

I just can't remember now if there was a gypsy in the group named Ronald.

Egg McBachelor

- Serves 1
- Cook time—about 8 minutes

1 egg

Butter

1 English muffin

1 slice of cooked ham (or deli ham)

Slice of American cheese

It doesn't get much easier than this. In a small frying pan, fry your egg in 1 tablespoon of butter, making sure to break the yolk. When egg is nearly done, flip it and turn off heat. Add your slice of cheese to egg. Slice the muffin in two and toast (optional). When the cheese is melted, lay the ham on a muffin half and top with egg and cheese. Top with whatever you eat on it: ketchup, mayo, or just plain butter. You can also try it with sausage, bacon, or whatever meat you want in the place of ham. You'll never need the drive-thru again!

What in Sam Hill Is That?

I met a French fellow from Mexico when I was living in Georgia. He was an odd sort of man. I never could figure him out. But the guy sure could cook.

It was difficult, at first, to understand Samjuan. He would start a sentence in French, end it in Spanish, and accent his words with a Southern drawl. If you don't think that was near impossible to understand! I don't know what he was doing in Georgia, but we became pretty good pals.

Samjuan always carried a baby food jar full of a heavy liquid that looked like pimple pus. I know where recipes are involved isn't a place to be talking about pimple pus, but the fluid was pretty intriguing. It was actually some concoction he learned to make from the Endolian cactus that grows wild in a small section of southwestern Mexico. Each time Samjuan took a swig of that pimple-pus-looking liquid, he would start speaking fluent English. I never saw anything like it.

But like I said, the guy could cook. And he gave me a little tip about cooking bacon that I've never tried but on which he swore in French, Spanish, and English would work. Samjuan told me to soak the bacon in Jack Daniels for about 20 minutes before cooking it. He said the liquor would penetrate the pork and keep the bacon from curling.

I think his notion held true because every breakfast wrap he ever fed me had bacon as straight as the pigs' legs that carried it.

I never tried his Jack Daniels philosophy for the simple fact that he drank what looked like pimple pus from a baby food jar. But I have made the breakfast wrap. And it's good. Give it a try, but I don't advise soaking your bacon in Jack Daniels. You might end up with a flash-fire in your pan. And rather than Samjuan, members of your local fire department might wonder what in sam hill you're doing!

Western Breakfast Wrap

- Serves 2
- Prep time—about 5 minutes
- Cook time—about 25 minutes

3 eggs

Butter (one tablespoon)

½ small green pepper (chopped)

½ small onion (chopped)

5 strips of cooked bacon

Salt and pepper

2 small tortilla shells

Salsa

In a medium-sized nonstick frying pan, cook bacon until done. Drain the grease and set bacon aside in a bowl lined with a paper towel to absorb any remaining grease. Return pan to the burner, add butter, and slowly melt. Remember, when cooking with butter, you don't want the heat too high, or the butter will burn and make your dish taste, well, burnt. After the butter is melted, add peppers and onions and turn the heat up slightly. Sauté (cook gently, stirring frequently) until the two soften somewhat. This will take about 3 to 4 minutes or 5, maybe 6. Keep a close eye on them.

Next, break your eggs and add them to the peppers and onions. Cook until the eggs are set and firm, stirring occasionally with a wooden spoon or plastic pancake turner so you don't scratch your pan. You want to make sure to keep your eggs broken up while cooking so you don't end up with an omelet.

When your eggs are cooked, turn off the heat and remove the pan from burner. If you have a microwave, place the tortillas on a plate, cover with a damp paper towel, and nuke about 30 seconds. If you don't have a microwave, empty your eggs in a bowl and warm your tortillas in your frying pan (about 1 minute on each side in a warm pan).

Place one tortilla on a plate and spoon 2 to 3 tablespoons of egg, forming a line down the center. Crumble half your bacon over the eggs, or lay 2 to 3 whole strips over the eggs. Add 2 or 3 tablespoons of salsa down the center as well. Fold one side of tortilla to the edge of egg, and bacon and the other half of the tortilla over the top of that.

Frita and Her Toast Are Not French

I'm not a real political guy, but the French have managed to ruffle more than a few feathers through their condemnation of the Iraq war. It doesn't matter to me whether you're for or against the war. Everyone is entitled to an opinion. We're not here to debate that.

What I find interesting, however, is the wave of outrage voiced toward the French by the American people. Following the incessant war protest by France, America came to know French fries as "freedom fries." French toast became "freedom toast." And French wine became toilet bowl cleaner.

How this toast got involved is a mystery. It's not even French. It's Finnish. I learned this little-known fact while vacationing in Finland in 1992. I met a girl there, Frita, and so impressed her with my stuffed mushrooms that she invited me to a night of dinner and dancing, which led to a morning shower and breakfast. (See guys, you gotta learn to cook!)

As Frita was preparing this toast, I said, "Wow, Frita, that looks like French toast." Her English was really bad, but her response translated something like, "Flense test! Hew der yew calit Flense test? Dis is Finnish test. Da Flense hast nuthikg te du weth dis test."

Her tirade went on for twenty-two minutes. I didn't get a whole lot out of it, save for getting a good tongue lashing, and the fact that it was Finnish "test" she was making and not French "test."

I don't know how, but the French must have really pissed off the Fins at some point in time and stolen this great toast recipe to boot.

I doubt that my discovery in the foothills of a small village in Finland will have any impact on French toast versus Finnish toast.

In fact, I'll finish this toast with Finnish vodka on the rocks.

I hope you enjoy my discovery. And if you need toilet bowl cleaner, there's some medium-priced Cabernet Franc at your corner liquor store.

Finnish Toast

- Serves 1
- Cook time—about 10 minutes

1 egg

¼ cup milk

A capful of vanilla (optional, but good)

A couple slices of bread

In a mixing bowl, add egg, milk, and vanilla and blend together. Spray your frying pan with a pan spray and heat. When pan is warm, dip your bread into the egg mix and cook until one side is browned. Flip and brown other side. Serve with butter or syrup.

Of Sake, Women, and Leftover Noodles

There's a small café called Norton's in the tiny town of Newt's Bluff, Nebraska, where, in 1983, I acquired one of the most unique recipes you'll ever taste.

This dish was a once-secret Chinese recipe crafted by the head chef at Norton's. His name was Lloyd. He was a small, gray-haired man who I guessed to be ninety-five or so, and an oddity in a Midwestern restaurant. He found work there in the early fifties after he was fired from his cooking stint at a chic Chinese establishment in Boston.

How he ended up in Nebraska is anyone's guess. He never said.

However, Lloyd and I used to talk for hours about everything else after the café closed. He always had a small bottle of sake (pronounced sock-ee) hidden in an empty flour sack at the back of the fourth shelf in the second cupboard behind the third counter. For those who don't know, sake is rice liquor that packs the punch of a pissed-off kangaroo. After a few sips of sake, Lloyd would first praise the Japanese for their winemaking prowess and then begin to talk about women and how he hated cooking Midwestern beef without peapods and watercress.

Lloyd loved women. He too was a bachelor. I think that's why we got along so well. I would tell him of the women I dated and what I cooked for them, and he would do the same. (His exchange was always a little shorter.)

One Saturday night as we sat sipping sake and swapping stories about simple silly songs we sometimes sang to socialize, Lloyd suddenly stood up and asked if I wanted a secret recipe he had created as a boy for his mother in his native China. "Gets girls." He beamed.

"Yeeesss," I slurred.

"World famous!" Lloyd exclaimed. "I cook, you write," he said, tossing me his food order pad and a pen.

Lloyd ran to the back of the café and soon returned with a bowl of cold spaghetti, a couple of eggs, some soy sauce, a garlic clove, and butter. I wrote feverishly as he moved with the swiftness of a Chinese cook.

When he finished, Lloyd handed me one of the most distinctive breakfast dishes I'd ever tasted.

I've never been back to Newt's Bluff or kept in touch with my friend. I will, however, occasionally buy a bottle of sake and reminisce about the times at Norton's and little Lloyd, the man who has now shared with the world an ancient Chinese secret—egg noodles.

Egg Noodles (Bachelor Style)

- Serves 1
- Cook time—about 10 minutes

1 cup of leftover spaghetti (no sauce)

1 egg

Butter

Soy sauce

Garlic salt to taste

Put spaghetti in a bowl and run warm water over noodles to help loosen them up. While they're soaking, melt a tablespoon of butter in a frying pan. Add noodles and fry until they begin to brown. As the pasta is frying, add a few shakes of soy sauce to keep moist. **Important**: constantly separate strings of noodles to keep from caking. When the spaghetti is nearly browned, add egg and mix well. When the eggs are cooked, splash again with soy sauce, and serve yourself a true bachelor's breakfast. If you have company for breakfast, simply double the spaghetti and egg.

A Roman Berry Picking

The origin of the word *breakfast* comes from the Roman Brake-Fast. The Roman interpretation meant, "Pause and put something into your belly before watching the lions swallow your fellow countrymen."

History states that Christians were fed to the lions for their belief in one God. I have no desire here to dispute that. However, there is a little-known secret that has never been discussed to my knowledge. That secret is in the form of a pamphlet that is now in the hands of an underground women's coalition in Saginaw, Michigan.

Although I don't know the full details, I was given a snippet of its contents by a lady friend who once held a high post in that coalition.

It seems that a woman named Cornelia led a movement in Rome's early years to deprive men of all things masculine. And I mean *all* things masculine. Cornelia hated men. There was no psychological evaluation done as to why she hated men, but according to my friend, key parts of the pamphlet reveal one possibility. It seems that a male companion, Juniperus, had agreed to break bread with Cornelia. Sharing half a loaf of bread was a sensual come-on that was common practice in ancient Rome. Well, Juniperus selfishly ate the entire loaf himself. This enraged Cornelia to such a degree that she lured Juniperus into bed with the promise of sex and, well, de-berried him.

Legend lives that is how the Juniper berry tree was born. BennWa, the god of berries, planted Juniperus berries out of respect for the mortal. So the next time you find yourself picking Juniper berries, please have a moment of silence in remembrance of the berryless Juniperus.

And words to the wise, guys, if you say you are going to break bread with a woman (i.e., spring for dinner) do so! Remember, "Hell hath no fury like a woman scorned or not fed."

It's a learning process for us, gentlemen. And it scares me how history tends to repeat itself. The berry picking is but one example. It should serve as a delicate reminder that women are special creatures, and they should be treated with care and with one eye open at all times.

With that said, keep both eyes open on this breakfast sandwich. It's a woman pleaser and will have your overnight guest wanting more.

Restaurant-Style Egg Sandwich

- Serves 1
- Prep time—about 2 minutes
- Cook time—about 8 minutes

1 egg

Butter (one tablespoon, it's marked on the stick of butter)

1 slice ripe tomato

1 slice American cheese

Mayo

Ketchup

2 slices of favorite bread

In a frying pan or skillet, slowly melt the butter. As with any dish calling for melted butter, melt slowly so the butter doesn't burn. When the butter is melted, crack the egg and cook gently over low heat. Be sure to take a fork, break the egg yolk, and spread it around a little bit. When the egg is fully cooked (you can tell when the clear part of the egg turns white), flip with a spatula or pancake turner. Lay the slice of cheese over the top of the turned egg. When the cheese is soft and mostly melted, remove the egg from the pan and place cheese side up on one of the pieces of bread. Top with the tomato slice. Spread a thin layer of mayo and ketchup on other slice. Salt and pepper to taste. When cooking for two, simply double the recipe.

Mushroom Cloud

The more I studied the mushroom for this dish, the more intrigued I became. I learned that average people actually make a living growing them.

Because mushrooms thrive in warm, moist climates, I headed south to learn more. My first stop was Cap, North Carolina. Fern and Stump Sotherland raised shiitake mushrooms. They had acres of old, rotting logs containing the tiny shiitake fungus sprouting from various holes drilled in the wood. The operation was impressive, extensive, and they made big bucks selling the shiitake mushrooms.

I found a portobello farm in Porthole, Georgia. Pam and Peter Nunce owned a farm where they raised these meaty mushrooms in much the same way. They cut down trees, drilled holes in the logs, planted the fungus, and made thousands of dollars harvesting and selling the portobellos that grew.

My knowledge of the edible fungus was mushrooming. There was, however, one more mushroom I'd heard about and wanted to learn more. Some called it the "magic mushroom."

My search for these "shrooms" led me to New Mexico. Unlike the other farmers, Randy Redcloud grew his mushrooms in his basement. Randy had several flower flats filled with fungus reaching for the hot lights above.

"Would you like to try one?" he asked politely. Remembering the wonderful mushroom dishes prepared by my earlier hosts, I graciously accepted.

Randy reached behind a pile of cinder blocks and pulled out a small baggie. "Here," he said, handing me a dried-out mushroom cap. "Go ahead, eat it."

"Aren't we gonna prepare a dish?" I asked.

"No cooking required," he said.

I thought it was kinda odd but popped the cap in my mouth anyway. I chewed slowly as we made our way onto his back porch. I didn't say anything, but the mushroom was the worst tasting, bitter fungus I'd eaten thus far.

As we sat and talked, my body began to feel a little peculiar. I turned to Randy to ask him where his market was for the mushrooms, knowing they couldn't be very profitable because of the way they tasted. But before I could speak, eight little monkeys appeared in the sand wearing sunglasses and top hats and smoking cigarettes. They danced around a giant shiny fish, flopping around in the yard. I gave a sideways glance at Randy, but his face looked like a car tire so I said nothing.

I turned my attention back to the giant shiny fish in time to see him swallow the last monkey and begin growing hair. He belched, focused his fish eyes on me, and in a deep baritone voice began to sing, "If I had a hook and line, I'd stick your cheek and drag you through the slime."

I flew out of my chair and past what should've been Randy. I say *should've* because sitting in the chair was a spotted lizard reading a Dr. Phil book.

Go ahead and try this recipe. But please, use a portobello and not a "magic mushroom." And if you see a spotted lizard reading a Dr. Phil book, get some professional help.

Portobello Morning

- Serves 2
- Prep time—about 3 minutes
- Cook time—about 25 minutes

2 portobello mushroom caps

4 eggs

Ketchup

1 cup shredded white or yellow cheddar cheese

Start by preheating your oven to 350 degrees. Next, take out the stem of your mushroom caps and wash the caps. Throw the stems away. Between two paper towels, soak up any excess water on the mushroom caps. In a buttered frying pan, scramble your 4 eggs. Do this by simply stirring the eggs until they're cooked. When the eggs are set, remove them from the heat. Now, take a cookie sheet and line it with aluminum foil. Put the 2 mushroom caps on the sheet and spoon in the eggs, covering the entire cap. Divide equally. Next, give each cap a good shot of ketchup (about two tablespoons each) and spread evenly. Top each cap with 1/2 cup (or more) of shredded cheese and bake for 15–18 minutes. If you don't like ketchup, try spaghetti sauce or salsa. This is a tasty way to start your day!

Can the Ham

Chris P. Bacon was a pig farmer who lived about a mile down the road from where I spent some time as a wee one in Hogback, Missouri. It was a privilege helping Bacon each morning before school fill the troughs with milk, stale doughnuts, and whatever else the town of Hogback threw in the dumpsters the night before. Bacon would spend about an hour each night driving around town collecting the food garbage to feed his pigs the next morning.

At 6:15 a.m. sharp, I would show up at Bacon's house and squeal with joy when those old pigs came running to slurp up the sloppy mix, snouts dripping and pig tails pumping.

I'll never forget one old sow. She was special. I'd feed her a jelly doughnut, and she'd chew and chew and chew, and just when you thought she was done, she'd spit out the jelly. It was the most amazing thing I'd ever seen. I loved that fat old pig. Bacon called her Can. I think it was because she had such a fat butt.

I had just turned eleven when one morning Bacon called me on the phone. He invited me to his house for eggs and toast before school. I hadn't seen much of Bacon since I stopped helping feed his swine about a year earlier due to more important things happening in my life, including puberty.

He had set a gracious table for being a simple breakfast. As a kid, I was impressed. He had his best milk glasses filled to the brim with fresh milk and topped with a sprinkle of cinnamon, a large plate adorned with two farm fresh fried eggs with the yellowiest yolks you could imagine, and a big old slice of meat, the likes of which I'd never seen before.

I pigged out that morning. It was one of the best breakfast meals I'd ever sat down to. Once I'd finished, I turned to old Chris P. Bacon and asked, "Chris P., just what was that fat old slab of meat that tasted like I was in two hog heavens?"

"Son," he said, "that was just old canned ham."

Enjoy yours.

Ham and Eggs

- Serves 1
- Prep time—about 3 minutes
- Cook time—about 8 minutes

1 canned ham

2 eggs

2 slices of bread

This breakfast is as American as dry roasted nuts. And because a fresh ham is hardly ever prepared, save for the holidays, a canned one makes this meal practical whenever the mood hits. Simply slice the canned ham to the thickness you want. Either microwave or pan fry until hot. Cook your eggs the way you like them (I like mine sunny-side up so I can slosh my ham in the yolk), toast your bread, and you're ready for a breakfast that will have you thinking you're in hog heaven.

Lost in Translation

I was on the Internet one night and found an intriguing site. The opening line of the Web site shouted, "How do I know if she's attracted to me?" I jumped up and down like a monkey ready to play. It was a Web site dealing with body language.

Bachelors are always seeking knowledge to counter the intuitive nature of women, a phenomenon that keeps men at a distinct disadvantage.

The following is a list of body language signals this cyber-guy said any date would supposedly portray to "cue me in as to her being attracted to me." He instructed how to read body language cues. His list went as follows: (1) "Pay attention to her eyes. One sign of attraction is when her eyes are open really wide." (2) "When you are speaking, she will lean her body into you." (3) "She will play with her hair and lick her lips before she moves toward you." (4) Lastly, this "expert" wrote, "How to know when to go for the kiss." His brilliant suggestion was, "She wants the kiss if when you walk her to the car, she lingers and keeps talking and looking at you. What you do then is go in, move towards her lips, and see what she does. Then pull to the side and give her a hug. This will create tension. If she then talks more, look at her, touch her face, and move in for the kiss."

I met Laura shortly thereafter at a wine-tasting party hosted by an acquaintance who married one of my ex-girlfriends. There was an instant attraction thing going on with Laura that most bachelors feel when their lonely, pitiful life is at a standstill. I asked Laura to dinner the following night and she accepted. I thought it to be a perfect opportunity to put into play my newfound "reading body language" skills.

The date went fabulously, so it seemed. I carried the list the Internet expert had prescribed and checked it periodically to see how the date was progressing. Everything seemed right on cue. At the end of the night, Laura lingered near her car and kept talking with me. (Tip number four.) With all the confidence of a bull let out of the barn in the spring, I moved toward her lips and suddenly pulled to one side and gave her a hug. She continued talking, and I touched her face and moved in for the kiss just as instructed. That's when all hell broke loose.

"What in Sam Tar's holy checkered creation are you trying to do?" Laura screamed, slapping my face with a right hand that packed a boxer's wallop.

"I was going to kiss you!" I exclaimed.

"What made you think you could kiss me?"

"Your eyes were really wide open when you were talking to me at the dinner table," I explained.

"My contacts were dry, you idiot," she snapped.

"But Laura, you played with your hair and licked your lips!"

"I was ready to pull my hair out because I was so hungry and we weren't being served," she quipped. "And my lips were parched. They couldn't even serve us water!"

"Well, uh, when we were talking at the table, you leaned your body toward me," I stammered.

"I have hemorrhoids, you insensitive jerk!" she snapped back. "I have to lean." With that, Laura climbed into her car and floored the gas pedal, pelting me with tiny gravel rocks that felt like buckshot.

Lesson learned. If you need some Internet coach to tell you whether or not a woman likes you, hang it up for a while.

Desperation breeds desperation.

If you find yourself desperate, try this biscuit and sausage dish. It will not only help calm the nerves, but you'll find yourself with a new vote of confidence to try it all again—sometime.

Biscuits and Sausage Gravy

- Serves 4 (or a hungry 2)
- Cook time—about 30 minutes

½ pound sweet ground sausage

1 package biscuits

2 packets (1.2 oz.) or a jar of "country style" (white) gravy

This one's pretty easy too. You can find premade biscuits in the frozen or refrigerated section of your favorite grocer. In one of the other aisles, you can find either packaged gravy mixes (about 1 ounce in size) or jars. Cook your biscuits according to the package directions. In a frying pan, cook sausage until done (no longer pink inside) and drain. In a saucepan, either heat gravy from the jar or prepare gravy mix from package, according to directions. Once prepared, add sausage and simmer about two minutes. Top warm biscuits with sausage gravy and enjoy one of the easiest yet most tasty breakfast dishes in the universe. Serve with either a fried egg or on its own.

LUNCH

A Fish Tale

Tuna boat. What an interesting name for a sandwich. I remember when I was a shipmate on a tuna boat. Well, it wasn't a real tuna boat. Well, it was a real tuna boat in a sense, just not a commercial tuna boat.

My friend Paco and I decided in 1992 to catch tuna for a living and sell them to various restaurants along the West Coast. Tuna was bringing big bucks. We were going to make a killing and get rich. We converted an old fifteen-foot powerboat into our fishing vessel. Actually, the only thing we did was strap a couple king-sized coolers to the stern. Both were packed with ice; one we filled with beer and the other was for fish.

I knew nothing about tuna fishing, but Paco assured me that he did. He came from a long line of tuna eaters, he said. That's why I bought the beer in return for Paco's help on the ocean. After all, it was his knowledge that was going to bring us a whale of lifestyle.

So, each day at dawn for nearly two full weeks, we would

motor out ten miles offshore and sit in the hot Pacific sun, fish net in one hand and a cold beer in the other. Paco guaranteed me this was the way it was done. But each evening we would weave our way back to El Stupido Bay with two empty coolers.

Late one night as we sat on the boat dock after another day of catching nothing but a big bad beer buzz, I questioned Paco about the lack of tuna in our boat. "Sharks," he responded resolutely. "We got us a big influx of sharks chewin' up the tuna."

I gave Paco a puzzled look. "I haven't seen any sharks," I said, scratching my head with the edge of an empty beer can.

"Course not," he replied, opening the top of the cooler. "When they eat that much tuna, they're gonna be nappin.' You see, they eat the tuna at night, and during the day they take siestas. It makes perfect sense. How much tuna could you eat before you got fat and lazy?"

"I don't know, but I'd like to find out, you bullhead!"

Paco felt around the cooler. "Hey, we're outta beer," he said, tipping an empty can.

I was being fed a line and getting as red as a snapper.

Now I never claimed to be the swiftest sardine in the can, but that night I finally figured out Paco didn't know shad about catching tuna. Oh, his generational line caught tuna all right—every week when it went on sale at assorted supermarkets.

No, it turned out old Paco just liked beer—free, ice-cold beer. He's lucky he didn't get his bass kicked.

We live, we learn.

Tuna Boats

- Serves 1
- Prep time—about 5 minutes
- Cook time—about 30 seconds

1 can tuna in water (6 oz), drained

Mayonnaise

½ small onion, diced (optional)

2 slices American processed cheese

2 hot dog buns

In a small mixing bowl, empty tuna and add just enough mayonnaise to make it creamy. You'll have to use your own judgment on this one, as different people like different consistency to their tuna. It's up to you. Once it's mixed, add your onion if you're doing onion. If not, you're set to go. Toast your hot dog buns in the oven at about 350 degrees, or broil them (if you have an oven, you should have a broiler setting). Or, option C is to butter both halves of the inside and heat them buttered side down in a frying pan until brown. Once they're toasted, remove from heat and fill with tuna. Top with a cheese slice and either broil or microwave until cheese is melted. Either way, it will take about 30 seconds. That's it!

Barefoot and Single in the Kitchen, a Recipe for Bologna Barbecue

Who knew what a wonder bologna can be? I remember as a kid down on the farm, when we had eaten all the sheep, chickens, cows, and pigs, bologna was nothing short of a delicacy. I would roll a dill pickle inside a piece of bologna and have a slice of heaven on earth. I remember the family sitting down to fried bologna sandwiches. We scrambled bologna with eggs and had bologna salad.

Wow, it's a treat just sitting here reminiscing. And this Bachelor's BBQ is a treat. You don't have to wish you were sinking your teeth into a tender, slightly seasoned lamb chop, or a meaty piece of zesty flavored chicken breast, or a nice, thick, juicy, black diamond steak, or even delicately simmered pork tenderloin.

No, no, no. Rich or poor, bologna has more.

But I've known people to turn up their noses at the very

thought of eating bologna. "It's beneath me," some would say. Others would retort, "Bologna is a poor man's meat without a whiff of sophistication." To these people I say, "Go suck an egg!" Bologna is nothing more than a cooked, smoked sausage made of cured beef, pork, or a combination of the two.

In fact, the Broods for the Betterment of Bologna Relations in Bismarck are credited with bringing the benefits of bison bologna to the forefront of the public's mind in 1902. It was only after the bison were near extinction that beef and pork were incorporated into the meat.

Through research, I found that bologna got its distasteful association in the early 1950s. It was during that period when North Korea invaded South Korea and started the Korean War. This is where it gets weird. North Korea worshiped its cows; South Korea revered its pigs. In an underground effort to provide meat to its fighting armies, those who were neutral in the war exchanged cows and pigs. Stick with me here—North Korea would send boatloads of cows down the Han River while South Korea sent boatloads of pigs up the Han River. Koreans to the north would butcher the pigs; Koreans to the south butchered the cows. A bologna plant was established on an imaginary border between the two fighting sides where cow met pig. It was a mutual plan that worked out well for both sides. The North Koreans ate well on stir-fried bologna, while the South Koreans feasted on hot and spicy bologna soup.

Try my bologna barbecue. If you're not completely satisfied, return the unused portions to the frying pan. There will be no refund of your ingredients, but your pet or neighborhood scavenger will appreciate the warm gesture you have to offer.

Bachelor BBQ

- Serves 2–3
- Prep time—about 5 minutes
- Cook time—about 15 minutes

½ lb. thin-sliced bologna (or deli ham)

1 medium onion (chopped)

1 cup ketchup

3 tablespoons vinegar

2 tablespoons brown sugar

½ cup water

Slice bologna into small strips or squares. Mix meat and onion in saucepan. Add water and cook over medium heat until water is cooked off and meat is slightly browned, stirring occasionally. Add ketchup, vinegar, and brown sugar and simmer 6–8 minutes. Serve in a hamburger roll or on toast.

Sour Note

I read recently where having a woman in the house helps you live ten years longer. With bachelor written all over me, I felt like I was missing out.

Being a proactive kind of guy, I decided to learn to play an instrument in an effort to attract a woman and add those ten years to my life. And it would be easy as I come from a family of players. My father played electric guitar. My mother played bass. Brother Rick, drums. Brother Dennis, keyboards. Brother Don, the field, but he eventually got married.

I decided on strings, as guitarists seem to be the screaming memes of music. I had the gift, and learning came quickly. When my fiery-fast fingers could finally fly from fret to fret, I phoned a friend who founded "The Flaming Foo Foo's." I asked if I could join the band on the nights they played any local bars. The Foo Foo's were famous for playing nursing homes and vets clubs. Nothing against either, but my motives were elsewhere.

When the band was booked to play a local nightclub in Indigo, Indiana, I got the call. The club was notorious for wild and crazy women. *Easy pickin's*, I thought. Ten extra years on a note.

I drove to the club that night dressed in tight leather pants, a tee-shirt two sizes too small, and enough mousse in my hair to start my own company. Nearing middle-age, I must have looked liked, well, just that. But I didn't care. It was life in the fast lane, baby.

On stage, I scanned the scene and smiled. Beautiful women as far as the eye could see. Silence hushed the crowd as the lights dimmed and the first few drumbeats boomed in the opening song. Just as it was my cue to strike the first chord, I leaped into the air like I had seen in the videos on TV. When I landed, however, my left knee popped and tight leather pants split wide. As I lay groaning, grabbing my knee and flashing the crowd my polka-dotted boxers, laughter erupted from the crowd. Someone threw a beer, and a woman shouted, "Are you pregnant or a fan of the local buffet?"

My band buddies dragged me backstage. As the smell of cigarette smoke and stale beer swirled, I could only shake my head. What in the blue blazes was I thinking?

Life in the fast lane came abruptly to a screeching halt. As for those ten years, I guess I'll play my swan song in the nursing home.

You don't need to live life in the fast lane to enjoy the following recipe. It's great for lunch or supper, or when you're looking to impress that special someone without a guitar in hand. I can't guarantee it'll add ten years to your life, but I can guarantee you'll love it.

Chicken Pot Pie

- Serves 2
- Prep time—about 10 minutes
- Cook time—about 30–35 minutes

1 cup of cooked chicken (cut up)

2 cups thawed, frozen mixed vegetables

1 can (10 ¾ oz.) condensed cream of chicken soup

½ can (4 oz.) sliced mushrooms (drained)

Chicken seasoning (optional)

½ cup of milk

1 cup Bisquick

1 egg

Another bachelor's favorite. Start by setting your oven temperature to 375 degrees. Next, in a small casserole dish, mix the soup, mushrooms, vegetables, and chicken. Add 4 or 5 shakes of chicken seasoning and mix well. In a bowl, blend all of the remaining ingredients until thoroughly mixed. Pour over chicken and vegetables and bake for approximately 30–35 minutes. The dish is done when the top turns a golden brown.

Courting a Lounge Lizard

Amber sat quietly in the corner of the Lizard Lounge in Tooten, Tennessee, one hot summer night not long ago. A few weeks earlier I had responded to an ad for a "space-aged" coat-hanger salesman. According to the Internet ad, these hangers were to revolutionize the way women hung their clothes. I was going to retire a wealthy man.

I stopped in Tooten, a tiny town of approximately 5,000, on

my way to San Francisco. I'd heard that both women *and* men in San Francisco were open to new experiences. These hangers were certain to be a hit.

I approached Amber that night, looking for a little companionship. She appeared genuinely lost and lonely. As puffs of blue smoke danced about her head, I asked Amber if I could join her for a drink. With a cigarette in one hand and a can of beer in the other, she nodded for me to sit down. I motioned to the bartender.

"What do you want?" the burly bartender shouted, swinging a wet bar towel over his shoulder.

I raised two fingers signaling for two drinks to be brought to the table.

"Peace this!" the bartender bawled, flipping me a single finger as he shifted his cigar in his mouth.

Somewhat embarrassed, I apologized to the woman. "I'll be right back," I said. Excusing myself from the table, I walked across the room to confront the bartender.

"I'm in town on business, and I would like to buy the lady a drink," I said politely.

"Lady? Amber?" A laugh emanated from his oversized gut like a roll of thunder. "Mister fancy pants, if you knew what was good for you, you'd run and never look back."

"Two beers, please," I repeated, shrugging off his comments. (What I didn't understand was that he was trying to tell me to *run* and *never* look back.)

Still laughing, he blew a putrid puff of cigar smoke in my face as he slid the two beers across the bar. "They're on the house!" he proclaimed. "The embalmer will appreciate me sending him business."

Shooting him a wary eye, I returned to the table and sat down beside Amber.

"So, do you live around here?" I asked, soon realizing the stupidity of the question.

Amber picked up her cigarette from the ashtray and drew

hard. "No, I live in Kansas," she said, exhaling, while at the same time sipping her beer.

I was just about to apologize for my ignorance when a hand the size of a large tortilla folded itself around my neck. I felt like a turkey wrap. Suffice it to say that if you've never met a biker from Tooten, Tennessee, pray you never do.

As I picked pieces of table paint from my teeth, Amber took another sip of her beer and tried to explain to the biker that I was a harmless salesman passing through town.

"Ya want what he's sellin'?" Mongol asked, reaffirming his grip on my neck.

"No," she replied flatly.

The bartender stood with the door opened wide as the last thing the biker saw was the soles of my Hush Puppies. As I picked pieces of porch paint from my teeth, I heard the rumble of a dozen more bikes on the horizon. Never one to let chivalrous behavior be the gateway to insanity, Tooten was soon in my taillights.

I've learned the hard way that companions don't necessarily have to come in the form of a female. Try pairing up with the following recipe. It's much easier on the teeth.

Italian Burgers

- Serves 2 (with leftovers)
- Prep time—about 5 minutes
- Cook time—about 20 minutes

1 pound ground beef

1 can tomato soup

1 cup water

Mozzarella cheese

> Form the ground beef into 6 patties and place in a large casserole dish. Combine soup and water and pour over patties. Top with cheese and bake at 400 degrees for about 20 minutes. Serve over pasta or on a roll. These are deceptively delicious!

A Foxy UFO

I'm not usually a very political guy, but there was a presidential candidate who, if he ever runs again, will get my vote no matter what. When Dennis Kucinich admitted to the world that he had seen a UFO in California, he was speaking my language.

I had my first encounter with a UFO in the early eighties. I was working in the U.S. Forestry Department in Utah and had attended a summer seminar as part of their work program. The UFO moved as a shadow outside the training room window. It was the most beautiful silhouette I'd ever seen. I was mesmerized by its sheer awesomeness. To my surprise, no one else had seen it. I never told anyone of my experience, wanting to keep it to myself. But when it happened again a few years later in the farmlands of Pennsylvania, I could contain my excitement no longer.

I have to point out that there are men—and I've met a few of them—intimidated by UFOs. Some run with fear; others stare, paralyzed by the realization that such a phenomenon exists. And that's why I feel it's important to bring this marvel to light.

It was a hot June early evening in 2002. The sun had barely set over the hayfield I was working in when the UFO I refer to appeared. I had just loaded the last hay bale on the wagon when a strange sensation overcame me. For reasons that remain unexplained, I looked to the west along a hedgerow that stretched for maybe half a mile. It was there, moving like a phantom, that I saw my second UFO. Flashbacks to my sighting in Utah and not investigating the phenomenon prompted me to climb into the tractor cab and shut down the engine.

Wonderment engulfed me as I walked across the field toward the spot where I saw the UFO. Goosebumps crept over the length

LUNCH

of my body as I made my way through the thin line of hickory trees and blackberry bushes and over a stone fence that separated my land from the neighbor's.

I followed the trail the UFO had left, marked by standing hay that had been knocked down. The path led me to an area just inside a parcel of woods on the north face of my neighbor's land, where it abruptly ended. My knees began to tremble. How could a fast-moving UFO maneuver in the forest? I stood at the edge of the woods, peering into the late afternoon shadows formed by the thick growth of trees and knee-high ferns. It was then that I heard it—a faint whisper. I quickly checked the tops of the trees for wind. There was none. Someone, or something, was calling. Suddenly, there was movement off to the left in a grove of pines. I rubbed my eyes to try to focus in the shadows. I saw it again.

I caught a glimpse of a silhouette as the entity disappeared deeper into the woods. I tripped over stumps and rotted logs trying to catch up with the phenomenon. But with swift movements and knowledge of the terrain, the visitor had left me breathless and turning the four corners of the compass.

It had vanished.

As I live, breathe, and write, believe gentlemen, believe; Unidentified Female Objects do exist. And they're crafty. They move with the swiftness and agility of a wild fox avoiding capture. It's little wonder the public laughed when Mr. Kucinich reported he had seen one.

I've now seen two.

Out of This World Barbecued Butter Beans

- Serves 4
- Prep time—5 minutes
- Cook time—about 1 ½ hours

2 (15 oz.) cans butter beans, drained
3 slices bacon
½ cup ketchup
¾ cup brown sugar
½ cup chopped onion

Slice bacon into one-inch pieces. Combine the beans, brown sugar, ketchup, and onion in a large bowl and mix well. When thoroughly mixed, pour into a greased 1 ½-quart baking dish. Spread the bacon slices evenly over the top. Bake, uncovered, at 350 degrees for approximately 1 ½ hours.

The Birds, the Bees, and Maggie

I remember well my first bachelor picnic. It was a special time with a special gal. It was when I first learned about the birds and the bees.

I met Maggie shortly after Millie, who was between Myla and Mary. On that particular Sunday afternoon, we spread our blanket in a small patch of yellow daisies near the edge of a tiny country pond. The day was perfect for a summertime picnic. I kissed Maggie on the cheek as I handed her a competently prepared club sandwich.

Turning her face to absorb the warm July sun, Maggie kicked off her shoes and wiggled her toes in the tiny golden flower petals. As she unwrapped her lunch, a lone seagull cried overhead.

LUNCH

Although unusual to see a seagull in a farm field, it added to the romantic mood that was stirring. I poured Maggie a small glass of red wine.

"He must be hungry," she said, delicately picking a small piece of bread from her sandwich. Maggie smiled joyfully, tossing the tiny morsel into the flowers as she sipped her wine. "This is wonderful," she whispered warmly.

I was heading straight for dessert when suddenly the seagull swooped and snatched the crumb without ever touching the ground. He let out a cry, and the quiet afternoon was quickly shattered by the piercing screams of dozens of incoming gulls. I threw my sandwich into the air in an effort to distract them. But the throw was poor, and my meal fell squarely on Maggie's head. Four seagulls descended on her; two of the birds got the sandwich and flew away, but two hung tough. Grabbing a six-inch pickled sausage, I managed to beat one of them away. The other bird, however, had his crusty claws knotted in Maggie's curly auburn locks and couldn't fly free.

Woman and bird screamed in unison. I yelled for Maggie to dive into the pond as the water would straighten her curly hair and help free the creature. She made a mad dash for salvation but stepped on a bumblebee that was sucking on a daisy. She screamed again. Grabbing her foot, Maggie hopped wildly to the water's edge and plunged bird-first into the filmy pool.

I breathed a sigh of relief when the seagull shot from the water like a feathered rocket. My breath stopped short, however, when Maggie shot from the water, gasping, firing a look as cold as a frozen fish fillet.

I met Marla shortly after Maggie who was between Millie and Myla…

Maggie's Club Sandwich

- Serves 1
- Prep time—about 8 minutes
- Cook time—about 10 minutes

2 slices bacon

1 slice American cheese

3 slices bread, toasted

Mayonnaise

2 leaves lettuce

2 slices cooked deli turkey breast

2 slices tomato

Cook bacon over medium-high heat until done. Drain and place bacon on paper towels to absorb any leftover grease. Toast the bread and spread each slice with mayonnaise. On one slice of toast, place the turkey and lettuce. Cover with a slice of toast, then the cheese, bacon, and tomato. Top with last slice of toast. Cut sandwich into four sections and use a toothpick to hold each section together.

The Tennessee Two-Step

There's something special about a warm grilled ham and cheese sandwich. I'm not sure if it's the melted cheese, the texture, or the woman behind it.

I was first introduced to the grilled ham and cheese sandwich when I was living in Tennessee with my then girlfriend, Mabelene. She was awesome, with hair the color of a nice, light cheddar cheese sauce and eyes as dark as two black olives. Mabelene stood about as tall as a stalk of sweet corn and had a body the shape of an early harvest butternut squash.

LUNCH

I was totally in love.

Late one night, after our second night of dating, Mabelene invited me to her cabin for a midnight snack. Our date consisted of helping her Uncle Earl peel a bushel basket of potatoes. Uncle Earl was a moonshiner. He said he was going to throw a party. Judging from the Mason jar that he was filling our glasses from, that was far from the truth. But that was all right. I liked Uncle Earl.

I sat slumped on Mabelene's couch that night, butchering the theme to the *Dukes of Hazzard*. "She's a good 'ole girl…gettin' down on tha farm." As I muttered, Mabelene hummed over the wood stove as she fixed our midnight snack. When she finished, she placed my sandwich on an old wooden stool near the couch. Mabelene gracefully sat down in an overstuffed chair and delicately placed her sandwich on her lap. What followed was an eating marvel.

I started to thank Mabelene for a wonderful evening just as her curled tongue made a long, slow, smooth motion along the length of the edge of the hot slice of ham on her sandwich. As her tongue retreated into her mouth with a gooey gob of warm, melted cheese, I knew where I was going to call home.

And I did for the next three weeks.

The fourth week into our relationship, however, Mabelene began returning home later at night—sometimes well past three in the morning.

One night, late, after helping Uncle Earl peel more potatoes, I propped my eyes open with two shot glasses and waited for my love to come home. "Oh, Mabelene, why can't you be true?" I stammered as she came through the door. She stuck out her tongue, flipped me the bird, and went to bed.

Just after noon the following day, I found a note taped to my forehead that read, "Have your drunken carcass out of my house by the time I get home. If you have doubts that I'm serious, Uncle Earl's gonna be doing some peelin,' and it ain't gonna be taters!"

With Mabelene's words written so clearly, I beat Uncle Earl to the punch and peeled that chapter out of my life. I can't wait for the next chapter to begin.

Mabelene's **Hot** Ham and Cheese

- Serves 1
- Prep time—none
- Cook time—about 7 minutes

2 slices of bread

1 thick slice of cooked ham

1 slice of American cheese

Butter

Simply butter one side of each slice of bread. In a heated frying pan, place one slice of buttered bread (butter side down). Lay slice of ham on bread and top with cheese. Place the other piece of buttered bread (buttered side up) on top. Cook until bottom side is browned and flip. Cook that side until browned and you're done. Not bad, huh?

Where's the Beef?

The first time I made one of these fat, plump, tasty burgers, I was living on the east coast of Florida, sand poor and eating once a day at a chicken joint that claimed they were serving real chicken. You know how you sometimes wonder if what you're eating is really what someone claims you're eating?

Yeah.

This chicken joint was tucked in an alley off the main boulevard. Stacked on either side of the entryway were bags of garbage that simmered daily in the hot Florida sun. I often wondered if the bags were left there intentionally to attract what might be going into the deep fryer. But I didn't care. It was cheap and what I could afford.

LUNCH

Back to the burger idea. I was riding in the back of a pickup truck one morning on my way to work in the sugarcane fields in the central section of the state. It was about an hour-and-a-half drive each way every day. During our first pit stop (the guys I worked with didn't believe in coffee; it was always beer in the morning…and afternoon…and night), I noticed a herd of cows grazing just off the side of the road. But these weren't just cows; they were beefers. Big beefers. The kind of beefers that make a fat, quarter-pound burger that drips with burger juice with every bite.

I found myself in a time warp not unlike the moment just before a cool rain on a hot, steamy summer day; my mind had left my body. I was transfixed on one particular animal. It stood staring directly at me, slowly moving its mouth back and forth, ingesting whatever it was chewing, slobber dripping from both corners of its face. I stared back, moving my mouth back and forth, ingesting nothing but air, slobber dripping from both corners of my face. I could taste him. I wasn't drunk, just outrageously hungry for something other than chicken, almost to the point of dementia.

I hopped out of the truck, and with the stealth of a creature on the prowl, I approached the animal, imaginary knife in one hand, fork in the other. I crossed the fence and was within a cow's breath of my prey when the drunks in the truck blew the horn long and loud. Startled, my out-of-body experience broken, I whirled around to pinpoint the source of the noise. Also frightened, the burly beefer snorted and scuffed at the thin layer of grass beneath his hoof. It was fifteen paces to the fence. I didn't make it.

After I got out of the hospital, I quit work in the cane fields. The rancher who owned the beefers, swallowing my story about how I was trying to save his herd from a wandering band of meat-eating land turtles, put me to work almost immediately—as the ranch-hand cook.

It was a day I'll never forget. Guess who exclusively came to dinner?

Swiss Burger with Mushrooms

- Serves 1
- Prep time—about 5 minutes
- Cook time—about 12 minutes

¼ pound of ground beef

1 tablespoon of butter

1 small can sliced mushrooms (4 oz. drained)

2 slices of Swiss cheese

1 Kaiser roll, or two slices of bread

Heat a nonstick frying pan and slowly melt butter. While the butter is melting, form the ground beef into a large patty as thick or thin as you want. Fry your burger to desired doneness. You can tell how done it is by cutting a small slice about halfway through and slightly separating the meat. When it's cooked to your liking, turn the heat down slightly, drain the grease, and return the burger to the pan. Layer the meat with as many mushrooms as will fit on top. Lay the slice of cheese over top of the mushrooms. Cover, and let the burger heat until the cheese is melted. It shouldn't take too long, so don't walk too far away. When the cheese is melted, place it on your bun or bread and dress it as you please with lettuce, tomato, onion, whatever you like. (You can also toast your roll by spreading some butter on the insides of the bun and laying butter side down in frying pan and heating over medium heat until browned.)

"Down in Louisiana Where the Black Trees Grow"

The bayous of southern Louisiana hold many mysteries. And no one knows these mysteries better than my friend Lefty. I used to be Lefty's right-hand man because Lefty didn't have a right hand. He lost his to an alligator snapping turtle—a big one.

Lefty used to love to venture into the swamps of Louisiana in search of alligator snapping turtles. "They are the crème de la crème of turtles to make soup," he used to say.

He doesn't say that anymore. Now he just uses beans.

Lefty, through the years, devised different cooking techniques because he only had one hand. For instance, when he wanted to crumble something like the chips in this recipe, he would put them in a plastic bag, throw them to the floor, and stomp them while dancing to some sort of jig in his head. To get tomato chunks, a rapid succession of whacks with a meat cleaver produced the desired result.

But the most interesting was Lefty's technique for getting edible-sized pieces of lettuce for his salad. Lefty would hold a head of lettuce, core side down, and pound the living tootoo out of it on top of his counter. When he was done with his assault, the core of the lettuce would fall out, and he'd reach inside and pull out bite-sized pieces. I never saw anything like it.

But all was not right with Lefty. He definitely had issues.

There was one point during our friendship when I drove Lefty to see Leona Laveau, direct descendent of the infamous Marie Laveau of New Orleans. Leona Laveau lived on the edge of Blackwood Swamp. I took Lefty there for fear he was going to crack because of his intense desire for revenge on the swamp creature that snatched his hand. The voodoo lady assured me that Lefty's troubles were nothing more than his left hand not knowing what his right was doing. In some perverted sense, that statement had implications.

Lefty had an immediate fondness for Leona. The two

swapped swamp stories for several hours while I poked sticks at the bats and snakes that were key ingredients in some of Laveau's voodoo potions. Leona sent us home that evening with a mixture of ground rat tail, an eye of a newt, and powdered crawfish claw. Lefty was instructed to mix a half-teaspoon of the ground rat tail and a half-teaspoon of the powdered crawfish claws in a glass of goat's milk each night for three nights before going to bed. On the fourth night, he was instructed to swallow the eye of newt while aloft in a tablespoon of chicken broth.

No one other than the voodoo lady knows how, but the concoction worked. Lefty was his old self once more. He never did hunt turtles again of course, but his life was filled with gentleness and a peace rarely seen in the swamplands of southern Louisiana. I heard that he eventually married Leona Laveau and that they now operate a voodoo specialty shop Web site out of their Houma home.

I'm going to check out that site as soon as I'm finished here. I think I'm in the mood for some Love Potion Number Nine.

Voodoo (Taco) Salad

- Serves 1 or 2
- Prep time—about 10 minutes
- Cook time—about 10 minutes

1 pound ground beef

1 packet (1.25 oz.) taco seasoning

½ cup shredded cheddar cheese

1 ripe tomato (cut in small chunks)

1 bag of salad lettuce

1 small onion (cut in small chunks)

A couple handfuls of zesty or cheesy tortilla chips

Salsa or sour cream

> Prepare ground beef mixture according to directions on the packet of taco seasoning. In a large serving bowl, crush enough tortilla chips to cover the bottom. Next, add as much lettuce as you think you're hungry for. There's no scientific formula here. Then add as much onion as you want. Top this with about a cup or cup and a half of ground beef mixture. Again, depending on how hungry you are. Next, add your tomato, followed by the cheddar cheese. Top with either salsa or sour cream, whichever you prefer.
>
> Your leftover ground beef mixture can be eaten in a taco shell, folded in an omelet for breakfast, or used for another salad tomorrow.

In a Pickle over Lunch

As I hung up the phone, I wondered what I had gotten myself into. I had just finished painting this ideal picture for my mother that life was great, super, fantastic. I was single, had a good job, lived in a great new apartment, and was eating exceptionally well.

But mothers sense things that aren't quite on the up and up. It's uncanny. You can tell them one thing and assure them of another, yet God's gift of intuition wins in the end. Mother told me she was on her way over, with Dad, to sit down to a gourmet lunch, "cooked bachelor style," as she phrased it.

I was frantic! It wasn't that I couldn't cook; the challenge was what I had to cook with.

As I paced back and forth between the cupboard and refrigerator, I chewed on a fingernail. In the upper cupboard, half a jar of peanut butter I used for mouse bait and some hairy strawberry jelly cried out, "Eat me, I dare ya!"

I rummaged anxiously through the fridge: some dill pickle slices with the centers eaten out of them, a few hard-boiled eggs that had begun to paint themselves with the colors of Easter, and a piece of ham with a cheese slice laid over the top, both with a tint of green. I quickly opened the freezer: one beef tongue, a year-old trout I'd forgotten about, and a freezer bag full of some kind of chunky substance. No idea what.

I sprinted back to the lower cupboard: mushroom soup, a can of tuna, a can of peas, a box of macaroni shells, and a half-can of mini sausages. I wondered how they got there. I picked up the can and took a whiff. I nearly lost my breakfast and threw the sausages to my dog, Butane. He swallowed them like candy.

Gathering all the cupboard ingredients I had on hand, I poured the soup in a saucepan and added the tuna and peas. Meanwhile, I started water boiling to cook the macaroni and called to Butane so he could lick the tuna can. He loved licking tuna cans. But Butane didn't come. It was then I heard a series of grunts coming from behind the kitchen curtain. Pulling the curtain to one side, I saw Butane hunching like he was ready to pinch a loaf. He let out another series of grunts, and I realized he wasn't gonna pinch a loaf—he was gonna puke. I quickly opened the sliding glass door and shooed him outside.

I stood watching Butane trying to determine what was going on with him when I heard the water boiling over on the stove. Running back to the stove, I slipped in a pool of dog slobber Butane left while salivating over the moldy sausages. "Why? Why me, Lord?" I asked, pulling myself up with the aid of a kitchen chair.

I turned the heat down on the water and added the macaroni to cook. While that was cooking, I quickly did the dishes, mopped up the dog slobber, and dusted off the drinking glasses. Twelve minutes later, I drained the macaroni and mixed in the soup, tuna, and peas. I was just finishing pouring it all into a nice casserole dish when my cell phone rang.

"Hello?"

"Hi, Son," my mother answered. "Your father and I decided to come over another time. The neighbors invited us to go bowling. I hope you didn't go to too much trouble..."

"No. No trouble," I replied, trying to disguise the relief in my voice. "I'll just put the filet mignon with mushroom sauce in the freezer for another time. Love you. Bye."

Try this dish, even if you're not under the gun from your mother. And a word of advice; check any hidden cavities in your dwelling for half-eaten cans of mini sausages. You can never be certain of late-hour antics when adult beverages are a part of your life.

Tuna and Noodle Express

- Serves 2
- Prep time—about 5 minutes
- Cook time—about 20 minutes

1 can (10 ¾ oz.) condensed cream of mushroom soup

1 can of milk

1 can of tuna in water (6 oz., drained)

1 can of green peas (15 oz., drained)

2 cups uncooked shell macaroni

If express is on your mind, this dish fits the bill. In a large pot, cook shells according to package directions. When done, drain and return to pot. Add soup. Mix well. Add tuna. Mix well. Add half the can of milk. Mix well. Add half the can of peas. Stir. By now, the shells should be nice and creamy. If not, add a little more milk—but not more than the 6-ounce can—and stir. Heat on stovetop for about 5 minutes and you're done. Serve with buttered bread.

From Russia with Love

Did you know that pizza isn't really an Italian dish? It's true. It's actually Russian. An old friend of mine, Pickael Crustachoff, of Pine Hills, Nevada, once showed me an official document containing the patent for the pizza dish submitted by his great, great grandfather Pizzael Crustachoff. It seems strange now, but decades ago you could actually patent a food dish.

According to Pickael, Pizzael came to this country from

Russia and spent most of his young life struggling as a vodka salesman. Pizzael immigrated to America with a vision of spreading the news of his native liquor among the American people. He brought with him fourteen barrels of vodka to pour as samples, hopefully to sway Americans into adopting the drink as a national beverage. However, vodka was not well received in this country. Beer was the beverage of choice, and as Pizzael struggled, he increasingly tapped into his vodka samples.

Pizzael had few friends in Nevada, but the ones he did have were loyal. Native to his country, they came to comfort him whenever he was home by drinking his vodka and sharing of their cold cuts. Cold cuts were a comfort food among the Russians. The realization that his vodka vision was a flop in America hurt Pizzael deeply. He was pained to see that cold cuts caught on while vodka bombed.

According to an entry in his diary, late one windy, January night, when all the cold cuts had been eaten and the last of his vodka consumed, Pizzael, depressed and fully loaded, mixed some flour and water in a small wooden bowl out of boredom. As he sang Russian songs out of key, he would reach into the bowl, roll small dough balls, and throw them against the cabin wall. One of the dough balls dropped haplessly on top of the woodstove he used to keep his cabin warm. The ball landed with a splat and formed a small pancake. Pizzael soon noticed that the pancake began to bake. He stumbled to the pantry and grabbed a jar of canned tomatoes he had brought from Russia. Opening the jar, he reached in, lifted out half a tomato, and dropped it on the pancake. His mind clouded by vodka but his instincts intact, he rushed to the icebox and returned with a handful of goat cheese, which he sprinkled wildly over the tomato. Pizzael swayed in amazement as the impromptu creation began to brown and bubble.

The rest, as we say in the cooking industry, is food history. It's a fact that's never been revealed until now, but we can thank Pizzael Crustachoff for what we now know as pizza crust.

Never doubt what you can do with a little vodka mixed with boredom.

Pizza for One

- Serves 2
- Prep time—about 10 minutes
- Cook time—about 12 minutes

1 package English muffins

1 jar pizza sauce (14 oz.)

1 package pre-sliced pepperoni (8 oz.)

1 package pizza cheese (8 oz.)

Preheat your oven to 350 degrees. Next, line a cookie sheet with aluminum foil. With a fork, carefully separate muffins into two slices. Use as many muffins as you want pizza slices. Place each slice on your cookie sheet. Next, top each slice with 2 tablespoons of pizza sauce and spread until covered. Layer each slice with as much pepperoni as you like. Top with cheese the same way, and you're ready for the oven. Bake until cheese is melted and golden brown (10 to 15 minutes). Remember, you can top your pizza with ham, olives, or those little fishes, anything you want. And give yourself a tip because you won't be seeing the pizza delivery guy!

The Ugly Side of Grapes

If you've never been on a wine-tasting tour through the wineries in upstate New York, you haven't lived. The scenery is spectacular, the wines outstanding, and the trip a memorable one.

And it's a great way to loosen up a stiff date.

I had been trying to charm Francene Faragut for the better part of three months. She was as cold as a flagpole in February. There was nothing I could do or say that would melt her frosty demeanor. I had all but given up on the idea of asking her out, when one day out of the blue she spoke. I don't know if she was depressed because her cat ate rat poison or her parakeet flew into a window, but she spoke. It was only to say "Hello," but it was indeed a breakthrough.

Time passed into late fall. Francene had progressed to the point where she was speaking full sentences to me. I felt as though I had arrived and that my time spent trying to woo her had worked. Feeling the friskiness of a newborn bull bison in spring, I invited Francene to a day of play. To my surprise, she accepted.

I had hit the jackpot. And, coincidently, I had hit the trifecta in the ninth race at Finger Lakes racetrack the day before and had cash to burn, so I rented a limousine to carry us on our tour. I went to such expenditure because I wanted to impress her, and I wanted us both to be able to enjoy the sweet nectar of the naked grape without climbing behind the wheel. (Who ever said bachelors are reckless?)

The date started poorly. Francene hugged the limo door as answers to my questions were acknowledged with only slight nods of her head.

But that all changed after our first winery stop.

It must be said that Francene was a skeletal girl, carrying just enough weight to hold her bones so they didn't simply fall into a heap. It took only that first sample of wine for her to begin to open up like a new book. As we climbed back into the limo, she slid farther away from the door and actually smiled at me. It was a short drive to the second cellar, and Francene seemed eager as the driver pulled to a stop. I had a new boost of confidence.

Inside, my date slammed her second sample and snuck another. Her eyes, only a short time ago remote and wary, turned mischievous. Her look should have been a harbinger of things to come but only registered in my mind as "lucky me."

Francene slapped my butt as we climbed the stairs to exit the building. Had I been a gentleman with pure thoughts, the incident would have left me offended. Instead, I smiled. Running to the limousine, we looked like two kids on a field trip. I had to instruct the chauffeur to drive on to the next winery, as he sat staring in the rearview mirror in disbelief at the transition in my date. I gave him my signature "thumbs up" as we drove away.

LUNCH

By the time we left the third chateau, Francene had turned sullen again. A dark cloud had blown through the limo window. My date began chattering like a pair of wind-up teeth. She told me that as a child she ripped the arm off her favorite doll, threw her hamster in the trash compacter, fell down the stairs while sleepwalking, and that she once ate a slimy, rotted apple she thought was baked.

I began to feel uneasy. I tried to get the driver's attention to signal him to turn around, but he was having no part of the breakdown that was occurring. I had read about the Jekyll-Hyde effect in college but thought it nonsense. I was now living it.

When Francene finally took a breath from her rant, I suggested we go to a restaurant where we could grab a coffee and maybe a slice of pie.

"My mother made mincemeat pies," Francene responded, wild-eyed. "She used squirrels from the backyard." The thought of dead squirrels mixed with the wine in her stomach must have been too much for her. She dropped to the limo floor and gagged.

I threw a penny and hit the driver in the right ear, finally getting his attention. Signaling for him to turn around, we headed back to Pennsylvania.

I never did see Francene again. But in the short time I spent with her, I'm afraid I may have triggered some deep-seated aggression that lay smoldering. I read recently in one of the regional newspapers that in a town not so far away, the local squirrel population was dwindling.

Although Francene was a twisted noodle, don't let this recipe fool you. It's good!

Noodles with a Twist

- Serves 4
- Prep time—about 5 minutes
- Cook time—about 30 minutes

1 pound of ground beef

1 can (14.5 oz.) chicken broth

1 can (10 ¾ oz.) condensed cream of chicken soup

3 cups broad egg noodles (medium size)

Cook your noodles according to the directions on the bag. When the noodles are done, drain them, don't rinse, and return them to the pot you cooked them in. In a frying pan, cook ground beef until it's done (no longer pink). Drain. Add the chicken soup to the noodles and mix well. Add the chicken broth and mix well. Add ground beef and mix again. Heat this mixture over medium heat for approximately 10 minutes, stirring occasionally. Salt and pepper to taste. The leftovers are fantastic.

Valentine's Showdown

Here we go again, a new year, another string of commercialized holidays to weaken the unsuspecting male species. Lighting the fuse to begin the slow burn in this litany of "What do you have for me?" celebrations is Valentine's Day.

And am I ready.

In a recently published article in *Chest* magazine, I was described as "a cynic with finely honed skills in the art of describing life, especially involving women." The course my life has taken, "especially involving women," leads me to accept that portrayal as a compliment.

It's no secret that, for me, cementing a relationship with a woman has been, well, difficult. And I'll admit that I may have gone overboard on a few occasions trying to do so. Take for instance Leela. On our first date, Leela told me in no uncertain terms that I made her physically sick. Although she took a cab home from the restaurant that evening, I convinced myself that it was a bad batch of green beans that did her in, not me. So, like any compassionate bachelor, I drove across town the next night and showed up at her door with a perfectly baked green bean casserole I had cooked with loving care.

She had me arrested.

Then there was Doreen. I met Doreen at a one-day Cooking with Care seminar on the West Coast. We hit it off splendidly. It was the proverbial love at first bite. We spent most of that night in my hotel room where we talked of egg noodles with a pepper-seasoned cream sauce and chicken breasts smothered in a warm wine and raisin paste. When I told Doreen I was a cooking bachelor who didn't have a pot to piss in but who had high hopes of one day landing my own cooking show, she politely excused herself from the room to go fill the ice bucket.

She never returned.

I spotted Doreen from the airport terminal window the next day in line, waiting to board a plane headed to Houston. When I ran onto the tarmac to ask her why she had disappeared so suddenly during our culinary discussion, she screamed to airport security that I was carrying a loaded tube of toothpaste.

They arrested me.

Nancy and Doreen are just the crust of the cupid pie. It's with them and the many others in mind that I offer the following piece of advice for all bachelors: trying to love a woman who scorns you is like licking honey from a thorn.

I've resigned myself to a new approach to women this year, and I'm kicking off my strategy this Valentine's Day. I've thought long and hard about women and how much it hurts each time I try to lick the honey. So I'm revealing my new methodology to pursuing the female persuasion for the first time here, in the hopes of saving at least one unsuspecting bachelor from being pricked.

I've designed a Valentine's Day card for use by bushwhacked bachelors that carries a simple yet powerful universal message. The cover of my card depicts a giant-winged pig with a colossal crabapple positioned pointedly in its mouth, balancing a pitchfork in his muddy hooves. He hovers over a massive bees' nest perched precariously atop a thorn bush. My crabapple-stuffed, pitchfork-carrying pig sports a bright red bow tied neatly on his curly little pig tail.

Inside the card, the message reads, "I receive no pleasure from your existence. I look at you, the way you dress, the way you walk, act, and think, and derive no enjoyment from any of it whatsoever. You satisfy no needs of mine, including sexual, emotional, and intellectual. There is no part of our relationship that profits me in any way. You're a basket case, and I'm only with you out of sympathy. Love, it ain't you."

It should be an interesting year...

Guys, if you've been jilted by the opposite sex, take solace in the following recipe. The dunking part is great therapy.

The Roast Beef Dunk

- Serves 2
- Prep time—about 5 minutes
- Cook time—about 15 minutes

Thinly sliced roast beef (deli)

Mozzarella cheese

1 medium-sized onion (fried)

Butter

Bread

McCormick Au Jus mix (1 oz.)

> Slice onion and fry in butter until it begins to soften. Fix Au Jus mix according to package. Butter one half of the bread, cover other half with cheese. Broil until cheese is melted. Remove from broiler and top with roast beef and fried onions.

Say Cheese!

The following isn't so much about the taco that we'll prepare later as it is about the various cheeses that go into making the dishes contained in these pages. The taco just happened to trigger my vast knowledge about cheese. Cheeses have a long and interesting past that few have the privilege of knowing. I thought this would be a good opportunity to explain how some cheeses originated.

First and foremost of these cheeses is the cheddar. We have two kinds of cheddar cheese for cooking—yellow cheddar and white cheddar. These cheeses are the products of the same variety of cow, the Cheddeschire. The difference in these two cheeses is the diets the cows are fed. Raised on the great spreading lands of Nebraska, the yellow cheddar Cheddeschire is fed a diet of ground corn meal and tiny onion bits; hence, the yellow color and strong taste. The white cheddar Cheddeschire, however, is fed daily a diet of ground popcorn and tiny onion bits. Same result, different color. The Cheddeschire cow is native to North America and is one of the most popular of the cheese producers.

It's when we begin to explore the producers of cheeses like the jalapeno that we start to understand the importance of importation enhancing our choices of cheeses. The Penosteen cow was imported from Mexico about 1860, as close as my research can put it. Producers of the hot Jalapeno cheese, the Penosteen are one ornery breed. Bred and raised in the heart of New Mexico, the Penosteen's daily diet consists of powdered hot peppers mixed in a combination of crushed oats and wheat. Hence, the fiery flare born to each batch of Jalapeno cheese. I mention ornery; it's not uncommon to witness a Penosteen chase down horse and cowboy after eating this peppery mix.

One of the more interesting of the domestic cheese producers is the Mozat. Records indicate that the Mozat cow was introduced to America as early as the late 1700s from France. The Mozat is a delicate breed raised exclusively on a nutritional regime of soft buttery crackers and coconut milk. The Mozat produces our light, pleasant-tasting mozzarella cheeses. You can find the largest concentration of these cows in Vermont.

The most disgusting of the cheese producers is the Cottage cow. Fed a strict base of vinegar and barley pellets, the Cottage cow produces a refrigerator favorite. I use the word *disgusting* because if you've never smelled a Cottage cow belch after eating vinegar and barley pellets, there's no other way to describe it. And to watch a Cottage cow being milked is also repulsive. The scene is not the fun, happy fluid stream of milk flowing from the cow's udders that you see in the movies and in picture books, with the happy little kitty waiting anxiously for a shot of milk. No, no. When you milk a Cottage cow, which has to be done by hand, you get a mass of lumpy, liquidly, chunky, mixed-up mess they call cottage cheese. These Cottage cows are one of Connecticut's best-kept secrets.

And you thought you knew it all.

Say cheese!

Hungry Man Taco

- Serves 2–4
- Prep time—about 10 minutes
- Cook time—about 10 minutes

1 pound ground beef

1 packet taco seasoning (1.25 oz.)

1 package shredded cheddar cheese (8 oz.)

1 package shredded lettuce (12 oz.)

LUNCH

> 1 small onion (chopped)
>
> 1 tomato (chopped)
>
> 1 package taco shells
>
> 1 jar of salsa
>
> Again, simple is what this book is all about. Cook ground beef and seasoning according to directions on taco seasoning package. When done, simply spoon into shell; top with lettuce, onion, tomato, salsa, and cheese. It simply doesn't get any easier. With the leftovers, create a great taco salad for lunch tomorrow!

Out of Africa

In my never-ending quest to bring new culinary dishes to the table, I recently took a trip to Africa to try to harvest recipes to bring back home.

Upon my arrival on the continent, I requested immediately to be taken to the Gabon region in the heart of the country's rainforest. It was there, in a prearranged meeting, I met with Bouku Balau Botswasu Buhoo of the Baka's pygmy tribe (I'll call him BB for short). BB had graciously answered an e-mail I had sent requesting the meeting to learn more about his tribe's cuisine.

My timing was impeccable. I arrived in the village just as BB's family was sitting down for lunch. We sat in a huge circle around a large cast-iron pot simmering over a hot open fire. As was tradition in the Baka tribe, BB's wife reached into the scalding pot with her bare hands and pulled out an item that looked hauntingly familiar and laid it gently onto a Kapuk tree leaf that served as a plate.

"Cane rat." A toothless BB smiled, watching his wife. "Tastes much like your prime rib." With one eye on BB and the other on his wife, I watched her reach back into the pot and remove two smaller items that also looked familiar. "Aagh, Tokay gecko." BB beamed. "Lizards. Most delicious." BB's wife handed me the leaf. "Eat, eat," BB said, pointing to my "plate."

I stared at the three pairs of lifeless eyes that had been boiled to the color gray. Tasting the half-dozen shots of whiskey I had on the airplane as they approached mid-throat level, I extended my leaf to BB. "It's tradition in my country to let the host have the first helping," I said, swallowing hard.

BB straightened with pride. "Oh, you generous Americans," he said, grabbing a gecko and dangling it by its tail above his open mouth.

"No, no!" I cried. "Take the big one!" But I was too late. BB dropped the lizard into his mouth, sucking in the tail like a string of spaghetti. The Buhoo clan clapped as BB smacked his lips in delight. Turning their attention to me, they waited patiently for me to follow suit. Trying to hide my disgust the best I could, I raised the remaining lizard by its tail and slowly lowered it toward my mouth. As all eyes were on the lizard, I shifted mine over mama Buhoo's shoulder and shouted, "Lion!" Everyone leapt to their feet, scattering in different directions, gathering spears and blowguns. In the midst of the commotion, I made a remarkable hook shot with the lizard back into the pot and grabbed the lifeless rat and tossed it over my shoulder into the dense jungle.

All panic passed before the Buhoos' once again assembled around the fire. "Oops," I said, making rapid chewing motions with my jaws, "false alarm." As the family sat back down, I dabbed the corners of my mouth with the tip of the tree leaf. "Most delicious, Mrs. Buhoo." Everyone stared for a moment, bewildered, scratching their heads before finally breaking into a smile.

"More!" BB shouted to his wife.

"No, no, no," I said, jumping to my feet. "I must go. I have a dozen more tribes to visit, and it's getting late. Thank you, Mr. and Mrs. Buhoo, for your hospitality."

BB started to wrap a rat to go, but I politely refused, stating that it was against American custom to eat rats on the road. BB nodded in appreciation. "Oh, you generous Americans," he said, handing me a coconut.

"What's this?" I asked.

"Filled with drink made from plant root bark," he replied. "Tis very hot today."

I thanked BB again and blew kisses to the Mrs. Two miles down the road, I drained the coconut, my throat parched from the tropical humidity. What BB failed to tell me was that his "fruity drink" was a psychoactive indole alkaloid, a psychogenic.

My plane ride back to America was in no uncertain terms a wild ride.

I was on this psychogenic journey when I dreamed up a couple different recipes involving mushrooms. This is one of them.

Mushroom Steak Sandwich

- Serves 2
- Prep time—about 5 minutes
- Cook time—about 12 minutes

1 can (10.5 oz.) condensed cream of mushroom soup

¾ can of milk

½ pound minute sandwich steaks

1 can (4 oz.) sliced mushrooms (drained)

1 tablespoon of butter

2 hamburger rolls

In a small saucepan, heat the soup and slowly add milk. Stir over medium heat until hot and add mushrooms. Meanwhile, in a medium-sized frying pan, melt your butter over low heat. These minute steaks come in 1-pound boxes with 16 steaks in each. Simply count out 8 of them for this recipe and throw the rest back in the freezer. When the butter is melted, break the sandwich steaks into pieces and add to the pan. It doesn't matter how big or small you break them. Cook the meat over medium heat until they are no longer pink. They cook fast. When they're done, drain the grease and return to the stove. Pour enough soup into the meat to nicely coat and mix well. This part is all your judgment. You don't want steak soup, just a nice mixture of soup to make a kind of sauce with the meat. Simmer for about 5 minutes to allow the flavors to blend.

In the meantime, if you have an extra frying pan, butter the inside of whatever kind of bread you have (hot dog buns, hamburger buns, bread), lay in pan, and heat until toasted. If you don't have another pan, you'll be fine without toasting your bread. It's good with or without the toasty part. You can have this sandwich with your leftover soup, or beans, or salad, or...

Bigfoot Blasphemy

I've always been fascinated with the great outdoors and its mysteries, such as Bigfoot. Ever since seeing my cousin Boo's size fourteen footprint in the snow, I knew other big feet must exist in the world.

My friend Ernie lived in Washington state, along the Yakima River, and constantly phoned to say he saw a Bigfoot. I told him I did too, and his name was Boo. Captivated by his continuous stories of the wild creature, I flew there for Labor Day.

Ernie and I packed our car for an extended weekend in the wild. Not only was I excited about seeing Bigfoot, or Skunk Ape as they call him in Florida, because of the awful stench people have reported after sightings, I was also anxious to try a few recipes I had cooked up in my head, concocted especially for ease of preparation in the woods.

The highlight of our first night in the woods was the pork chops with hot pepper sauce, brown sugar, and beer simmered slowly over an open fire. The meal was fantastic. We sipped a second twelve-pack after dinner with our noses to the wind waiting for any signs of Bigfoot. We went to our tent near midnight somewhat disappointed but feeling good in the great outdoors.

I awoke around 2:00 a.m., my nostrils burning from one of

the worst smells I've ever inhaled. My head still swimming in barley and hops, I bolted upright surmising that a Bigfoot was nearby. I was just about to shake Ernie awake when a blast of gas in his sleeping bag gave pause for cause.

"Ah, Ernie!" I mumbled. I stepped outside to refresh my lungs and refuel the fire.

No sooner had I sat down to enjoy the fire when a high-pitched scream pierced the night. My heart beat double time. I waited on the edge of my seat, listening intently. "Eeeee!" echoed in the dark. I burst into the tent trying to waft the smell and awaken Ernie.

I violently shook him, triggering another blast of gas. "Ernie, wake up! I heard Bigfoot!"

Ernie shot out of his sleeping bag, immediately grabbing his nose. "Phew, yeah, I smell him."

"That's you, you idiot. Come on!"

Ernie quickly followed me outside. "Man, it's cold out here," he whined, shivering in his boxers.

"Shhh," I insisted. "Listen."

Again, "Eeee!"

"Come on. It's coming from over here!" I grabbed a burning stick for light. We cautiously crept for fifty yards when we heard another scream.

"Up there behind that clump of trees," I said softly.

In a small clearing a short distance away, a lone tent silhouetted the night. We stood horrified as a hulking shadow rose and fell in the pale glow of light emanating from inside. Another shrill scream.

"Bigfoot!" Ernie gasped. "He's mauling a woman!" Ernie grabbed a maple branch the size of a leg and ran toward the tent, yelling as if speaking in tongues. As Ernie reached the side of the tent, I could see the hulking figure inside turn toward him.

Whump! Ernie's aim was true, and the giant fell in a clump. Another scream. But this one sounded…different.

As my mind raced to differentiate the two distinct pitches

of sound, a lump formed in my throat. My suspicions were confirmed when a naked woman darted from the tent and disappeared into the brush.

Ernie peeked inside the tent and dropped his club. He turned toward my direction, eyes bulging, his mouth hanging like a stretched rubber band. I could see him mouth the words, "Oh no."

We learned two days later that poor gent in the tent suffered a mild concussion from Ernie's whack with the stick, but that he'd be all right.

As for Bigfoot, well, I brought Ernie back east to meet my cousin Boo.

To satisfy the Bigfoot hunger in you, the following recipe is sure to fit the bill. It packs a man-sized wallop for one sitting or two.

Taco Beef and Noodle on a Bun

- Serves 2
- Prep time—about 8 minutes
- Cook time—about 15 minutes

1 box macaroni and cheese

1 lb. ground beef

¼ cup milk

¼ cup butter (margarine)

1 packet taco mix

4 slices cheese

4 hamburger buns

Fix macaroni and cheese according to box directions. While the macaroni cooks, brown ground beef until no longer pink. Drain fat and add taco mix. Place cheese on bun, cover with macaroni and cheese. Top with taco beef.

SUPPER

Love Ain't a Walk in the Park

Brenda sat reading on a bench during a quiet, sunny afternoon in a wooded park in downtown Cheeker's Bluff, Montana. I knew her name because she was a friend of a guy who worked for the brother of the boss who owned the sanitation company that cleaned the park who happened to be my beer buddy.

I watched Brenda every day during that month of August as she enjoyed her lunchtime reading, soaking in the summer sun. She always had a book in hand, alternately reading and feeding the little gray squirrels that bounded about her feet looking for handouts.

When you're a bachelor, and certain situations involve a woman, you do what you have learned to seize a moment; whether from watching television, reading books, or listening to married friends, you draw upon past understanding. And buried somewhere in the recesses of my mind, I knew a dog would win the heart of this woman (unlike a small child in a grocery store).

As usual, Brenda sat reading this particular afternoon, casually tossing a cracker now and again to the colony of squirrels that had become her friends. I climbed out of my car and nonchalantly strolled to the passenger side where Peanut sat anxiously waiting, panting, and eager to explore the park. Peanut was a mixed breed I had rescued from the animal shelter the day before with this day in mind. No one at the shelter was sure what mix he was, but they promised he was a darling dog women would adore—a real killer, the guy assured me with a wink.

I hooked Peanut's leash to his collar and wiped the slobber from the dashboard. Peanut was bigger than the name would suggest for a dog. He was more the size of a goat. I checked my hair in the side-view mirror, gave my pal a pat on the head, and began the leisurely walk through the lush green grass toward the park bench. Peanut tugged hard at the leash as we headed for my princess in paradise.

As we approached the bench, Brenda looked up and gracefully folded her book. "Oh, what a pretty dog," she said as we drew near.

"Why, thank you," I responded, again patting Peanut's head. I was beaming over the fact that I was a genius.

"I just love animals and—" Brenda's words were broken like a bad baseball bat as Peanut pounced on the crackers and quickly turned them to crumbs. Rattled, Brenda darted behind the bench as Peanut barked wildly at the empty cracker wrapper. I jerked his leash to settle him down; the look I got in return read "skin." I dropped the leash and jumped to join Brenda behind the bench.

Peanut was in a state of pandemonium.

From out of nowhere, a belligerent young squirrel made a mad dash toward a crumb in the grass.

Brenda threw up a hand in horror.
I turned my head.
Peanut choked on the tail.
Brenda bolted.
I sobbed.
Peanut puked.

I never did see Brenda again. The incident, however, spoke volumes for television, bad books, and married friends.

Although I had lost at potential love yet again, the comfort of the kitchen pulled me through. But you don't have to be a victim of love to enjoy these chicken quesadillas. They're delicious no matter the mood you're in.

Chicken Quesadilla

- Serves 2
- Prep time—none
- Cook time—about 5 minutes

Two large flour tortillas

Grated cheese (mild or sharp cheddar)

1 cup diced chicken (cooked)

Butter or olive oil

Heat butter or oil in frying pan over medium-high heat until hot. Add one tortilla. Flip after 10 seconds. Continue to flip until air pockets begin to form in the tortilla. Turn heat to low. Sprinkle cheese and half a cup of diced chicken over tortilla surface. When the cheese is melted, use a pancake turner to lift one side of the tortilla and flip over to the other side, much like making an omelet. Remove from heat and serve with salsa or sour cream.

Boared to Death

Razor Back, Arkansas, is home to my latest recipe, the Three Piggy Pork Sandwich. Orn Norville, an eighty-eight-year-old bachelor from the bogs of Razor Back, shared with me his secret recipe when I ran moonshine with him in the late 1990s. In addition to selling liquid fire, Norville also hunted wild pigs and sold the pork to local markets in Polk County. I'm sharing this recipe because Orn is no longer with us. He was attacked last year by a wild boar.

For poor Orn, being bored to death brought new meaning.

Orn was an intriguing character with eyes the color of mud and long, greasy, paper-white hair. Not that Orn was an unclean man, quite the contrary. He bathed regularly in Poopot Swamp. His least attractive feature, however, *was* his hair. When he skinned the boars he shot, Orn liked to scrape the fat from their hides and fashion a kind of hair gel made of pure hog fat mixed with a little swamp water. He combed it with care through his long, white strands. He said it made him look sexy.

You can imagine the kind of women hog fat attracted.

But I liked old Orn. He never judged anybody, and he would give you the hog's hair off his back. (He only had one shirt.) The little bitty pig curls growing in spotty patches really did look like hog's hair, and he once tried to get me to grease them.

"When pigs fly!" I squealed.

Under his coarse exterior, Orn had a compassionate characteristic that swam with the booze in his veins. One night, as we sipped moonshine fresh from the still, Orn, out of the blue, blamed his mother for his being a bachelor. As a child, he said, she would often recite the tale of the Three Little Pigs. Sometimes two or three readings a night, he said.

He thought that was the most terrible tale ever told.

But Orn never heard the true version of the story. His mother, a little touched in the head, changed the narrative. Her account involved three brick houses to keep all the pigs safe and an old, gray, asthmatic wolf that smoked cigars, drank gin, and wheezed when he breathed. Orn thought it was completely callous that the three little pigs never let that sickly wolf into their homes. The little porkers should have welcomed him in with open pigs' feet for a gin and tonic and an inhaler, he thought. Instead, he said, that poor wolf had to huff and puff and hack and wheeze to try to get in.

Orn said he would often cry during his mother's recitation

because he thought that surely the wolf would suffer lung collapse. He despised those little pigs for that. I guess that's why he grew up peeling pig hides for a living.

As for women, well, he never wanted to hear the story of the Three Little Pigs again. And since his mother recited the account religiously, he thought all women did. Yeah, he was a little twisted in that sense, definitely his mother's son.

But there's no twisting this recipe. It's good.

And if you don't like it, you can huff and puff…

Three Piggy Pork Sandwich

- Serves 2
- Prep time—about 2 hours
- Cook time—about 3 hours

1 pound pork roast (cooked)

3 cups shredded cabbage

1/3 cup sugar

1/2 cup mayonnaise

Italian salad dressing

2–3 hoagie rolls

Butter

My leftover pork came from a chunk of meat I cooked the night before. If that's the route you want to go, simply put your pork in a Crock-Pot with a couple cups of water, cover, and cook on medium heat for 8 or 9 hours or overnight. Or you can bake the roast by placing the pork in a roasting pan with 2 or 3 cups of water. Cover and bake at 350 degrees for 2 ½–3 hours, or until juices run clear when roast is poked. Once the meat is cooked, remove from heat and let cool.

Meanwhile, add cabbage to a large mixing bowl. The easiest way to get shredded cabbage is to buzz down to the supermarket and head to the produce section. There you should find shredded cabbage packaged for coleslaw. Or, if you're up for it, shred your own. Either way, once your cabbage is in the bowl, sprinkle the sugar evenly over top, cover with plastic wrap, and put it in the fridge for about 2 hours to allow the sugar to melt through the cabbage.

Now, if your roast is cool enough, with your fingers or a fork, pull off enough meat for 2 or 3 sandwiches and put it in a small mixing bowl. Pour enough Italian dressing in the bowl to coat the meat well when stirred. Cover and refrigerate for about 1 hour. When the cabbage is ready, add mayonnaise, mix well, and return to the fridge. After draining excess dressing from the meat, place it in a frying pan and warm through. Butter both sides of a roll and broil or brown in pan. Add meat, top with coleslaw, and enjoy. Enjoy the leftover coleslaw on its own and the leftover meat on sandwiches the next day.

East Meats West

When a singer names himself after a dinner item, you know it has to be good. Meat Loaf is one such instance.

But meatloaf was made popular long before the singer rode the name to stardom. In fact, a Chinese immigrant bricklayer in New York City in 1925 first brought meatloaf to light.

As the legend goes, and I've done the research, Mi Lo Fu came to the United States in the early 1920s. Fu learned his masonry trade in the Orient and brought his skills west to help support his family back home in his native village of Lai One Hi.

Fu was an astute worker. He put to shame other immigrants on various building projects and soon became legendary in New York City for his artistry in laying brick. He constructed landmark buildings including the Block Four House and the Block Five House. In addition to his masonry skills, Fu was revered by the city's elite as a cook extraordinaire, due mostly to his quick adaptation to western ways of cooking. Minus the rice vinegar and peanut oil of his native land, Fu quickly learned to create dishes utilizing fresh meats from the local stockyards.

Mi Lo Fu quickly made a name for himself in the inner circles of New York, creating food dishes and landscapes beyond compare. That in turn created a jealous buzz in Chinatown, despite his good intent. While others in the small community eked out a living surviving on beans and rice, Fu, due to his diligence and hard work, was paid handsomely and rewarded many times over with free meats and building contracts.

However, his arduous work and long hours eventually caught up with him. One wickedly hot summer afternoon, as the simmering sun scorched the city streets, Fu, atop a second-level building he was helping construct, prepared a ground beef dish for lunch with the intent of taking it to a local baker's shop to cook and offer to the contractor who had awarded him work on the project. But exhaustion floored Fu. Tired, barely able to move, Fu left his creation lying on a building brick. Nearly three hours passed when his fellow workers, smelling the aroma of ground beef baking in the summer sun, discovered Mi Lo Fu fast asleep in a pile of cool sand.

Excited cries from jealous coworkers echoed for a city block. "Mi loaf! Mi loaf!" A crowd soon gathered. The city's local hero was slumbering, and an envious community of immigrants was rejoicing, "Mi loaf! Mi loaf!"

The workers quickly gobbled up the bricklayer's lunch as he lay in deep sleep.

Records don't document the fate of Mi Lo Fu. What we do know is that the excited cries of "Mi loaf, Mi loaf" and the dish Mi Lo Fu created eventually became meatloaf.

The rest is ground beef history.

Meatloaf

- Serves 2–4
- Prep time—about 15 minutes
- Cook time—about 1 hour

1 pound ground beef

1 egg

1 small onion (chopped)

½ cup of bread crumbs

½ cup of milk

1 green pepper (diced)

Ketchup

Worcestershire sauce

Garlic powder

Preheat your oven to about 375 degrees. In a large mixing bowl, add ground beef and egg and mix well. Add your onion, bread crumbs, milk, green pepper, and mix it again until it looks fully blended. Add 4 shakes of Worcestershire sauce and 5 shakes of garlic powder (or salt) and mix again. Put mixture in a meatloaf pan (if you have one) or a small 9 x 11 casserole dish and spread out the mixture until it looks uniform (the same thickness). Top with as much ketchup as you want and spread it evenly. Some people like a lot, others not so much. Remember, you're a bachelor. It's your call. Bake approximately 45 minutes to an hour, depending on the cooking dish you use. You'll know it's done when the ground beef is no longer pink. Simply cut into it after 45 minutes. If you see pink, cook it another 15 minutes. You can't go wrong. Any leftover meatloaf makes great-tasting sandwiches for future meals.

It's Miller Time

People have often asked me, "Don't you ever want to settle down with a nice woman and create a happy home?"

I've responded to the question so regularly that it actually began to depress me. In a knee-jerk reaction to the most recent inquiry, I thumbed through the Yellow Pages in search of help. Dr. Sam Lithguard had a beautiful block ad on page 107 depicting a man in a straightjacket. The caption read, "If you're not committed, you're nuts!"

Brilliant, I thought, and made the appointment.

I was somewhat shocked when I showed up at my scheduled time to learn that Dr. Sam was a woman—a beautiful woman at that.

If you have never had your head examined, there really is a leather couch. Dr. Sam, in a womanly fashion, kindly asked me to remove my shoes and get comfortable. I was used to that. *This is going to be all right,* I thought. As she read my mental makeup in her feedback form, I tucked a hole my big toe had made in my sock between two other toes to conceal it and nestled into the deep comfort of the couch.

"Terry, according to the answers you gave on my questionnaire, you have intense feelings associated with disruptive degradation and despondency over a lifetime of curious exploits that have culminated into a reactionary frame of mind."

"I guess so," I answered sadly, wiping a tiny tear from my eye.

"Tell me what you think of women," Dr. Sam continued.

I quickly sat upright, my big toe popping from its hole. "I love women," I said, beaming. "Women are the salt of the earth; the pickle that makes man pucker; the bun that holds braised beef; the mayonnaise that makes egg salad. Oh, Dr. Sam, women are special."

"Is there a reason why you have never married?"

She was beginning to press my buttons, and I could feel her fingers pushing them. "It's like this hole in my sock." I wiggled my toe, trying to gain back control. "What do you think about this hole in my sock?"

"Well, it looks like your sock could use some mending," Dr. Sam answered softly.

"Exactly!" I cried, jumping from the couch. "This is my holy sock. It can't be desecrated by a needle and thread because I don't have someone saying, 'Your sock could use some mending!' This sock has been faithful to me, and I don't have to fear waking up some morning to find it not here because someone didn't like it and discarded it like some nasty old cat. This sock has been a blessing through the many miles I've walked in its glory. The heavens will rain fire before this sock is mended, leaving me finding myself missing it because it's gone!"

"Mr. Miller, are you all right?"

"No. I think I need a beer," I answered as I closed the door behind me.

That was the last leather couch I ever laid upon.

And to this day, I hold dear my holy sock and all the misguided meaning behind it.

And I hold dear this special barbecue chicken. I didn't need a shrink to come up with it, and it's great eating sitting on the living room couch. I think you'll agree.

Bachelor's Barbecue Chicken

- Serves 4
- Prep time—about 15 minutes
- Cook time—about 1 hour to 1 ½ hours

Four chicken halves

1 cup oil (vegetable or canola)

2 cups vinegar (white or cider)

2 eggs

½ cup salt

3 tablespoons poultry seasoning

3 teaspoons pepper

You don't need a shrink for this one. For the tastiest chicken, this sauce should be made (but it's not necessary) the night before your cookout and the chicken marinated in the refrigerator overnight. Mix all ingredients in a blender for approximately 2 minutes. Marinate chicken for an hour. When your charcoal is ready for cooking, place chicken on grill and begin. I like to turn my chicken every 5 to 7 minutes, basting the meat with leftover sauce each time I turn it. You'll want at least a six-pack, as this is a lengthy process, but well worth it.

Shotgun, Shells, and Sausage

There's nothing worse in a man's life than being dumped by a woman. And there's nothing more embarrassing than being dumped by a woman because she smelled a rat.

My little Lulu love nest unraveled in the spring of 1989. I was living in Lovetville, Louisiana, at the time, well into my bachelorhood and looking for a mate. Lulu was a librarian. We met while I was researching local recipes involving alligator meat and tomato paste.

Lulu moved into my small house on the bayou shortly after our three-month anniversary, at first bringing only a few dishes. We were as happy as two carrots in a stew.

Late one night, as she was rearranging my bookshelf in accordance with the Dewey decimal system, I noticed a large hole in my kitchen floor behind the refrigerator. I knew the signs of the intruder: Lulu had relayed to me her perpetual fear of rats.

Not wanting to risk my relationship over a rodent, I sent Lulu to her mother's for an overnight stay, explaining that I wanted to surprise her with an extravagant undertaking.

That night I lit a candle and crawled under the kitchen table with my double-barreled shotgun, waiting for the beady-eyed rodent. It was nearing ten o'clock when the rat charged from his hole; I swear he was the size of a meatloaf. I squeezed the first trigger. The rat was well clear of the blast, but Lulu's dishes weren't. In the candlelight, I saw fragments of white, green, and blue; I think the blue was a remnant of her good ones.

As the last particle of glass bounced across the floor, the rat pranced into the open, seemingly knowing who had won the first round. I quickly cocked the other hammer. But in my excitement to bump him off, I banged the table when I raised the shotgun barrel. The jolt toppled the candle, hot wax pouring into the back of my boxers. As I screamed, I squeezed the other trigger, blasting a hole square in the center of the refrigerator. Beer, egg yolk, and spoiled milk oozed from the holes.

Lulu came home early and turned on the lights just as the last curd of milk hit the floor. I was pulling a hardened stream of wax from my butt when I heard the shriek. The look of horror on Lulu's face upon seeing her shattered plates matched anything she could have expressed at seeing a rat.

I don't know what ever happened to Lulu. Before I left for the burn unit of the local hospital, I told her I was sorry and that I should have told her we had a walking meatloaf in the house. She told me she didn't give a rat's rear end. I came home and she was gone.

The lesson I learned is that two rats don't make a right.

Sausage and Shells

- Serves 2 (with leftovers)
- Prep time—zero
- Cook time—about 30 minutes

1 lb. box macaroni shells

1 lb. pork sausage (hot or sweet)

1 lb. 10 oz. jar of spaghetti sauce

> We love simple. Cook half the box of shells according to box directions. When cooked, drain and return to pot. In a medium-sized frying pan, cook sausage until done (browned and no longer pink). Drain fat and add to shells. Add the sauce, mix well, and heat for 5 to 7 minutes until warmed through. Dinner à la Monday.

Cabbage Patch Cooking for You and Your Doll

The cabbage is a somewhat curious food. Bred from a leafy wild plant found in the Mediterranean region around 100 A.D., the cabbage head is the only part of the plant that is normally eaten.

Cabbage is often prepared by boiling, usually as part of soups or stews. But for me, nothing hits the palate the way a ham and cabbage combination does.

I first discovered this bachelor's delight when my fourth girlfriend, Camilla, left me for a job overseas as a gorilla guide in the Congo. The move left me on all fours, but I eventually recovered. Before Camilla went ape, she used to tell me how her grandmother would boil ham and cabbage on cold winter nights in the mid-1950s and how much she enjoyed it.

It's a dish that stands to this day for one or two at dinner. And it's a dish you don't have to have a degree in cooking to prepare.

One word of caution concerning ham and cabbage: If you have your girlfriend—or hope-to-be girlfriend—over for this dish, casually place one Beano tablet on the table just above her fork before eating. You can explain to her that it's a mineral supplement to help fortify the dietary fibers contained in cabbage.

And it wouldn't be a bad idea if you ingested one yourself. Cabbage has been known to produce noxious gases that could potentially ruin a romantic evening. Trust me. I cook and communicate through experience.

Ham and cabbage plus Beano equals a night of delicious food that will have her back to sample your next recipe.

She'll love you for it.

Bachelor Ham and Cabbage

- Serves 4
- Prep time—about 5 minutes
- Cook time—about 7 hours

1–1 ½ lb. ham (approximately)

2–3 pound head of cabbage (approximately), quartered

Again, simplicity is what we're all about here. Haul out your Crock-Pot and fill with 4 or 5 cups of water. Drop in the ham. Set the heat on 3 or 4. Pull a couple layers of leaves off the cabbage and discard. Wash what's left. With a large knife, cut it in half. Next, cut each half in half again and drop into Crock-Pot. That's all you do! Put the cover on and leave it alone for 6 or 7 hours. When the ham falls apart and the cabbage is tender, it's done! Let's ham it up! Again, guys, don't be afraid to cook this for yourself. The leftovers will last up to 4 days in the refrigerator. That's two less lunches or dinners you'll have to cook.

Baby Blues

I love all creatures with hair, without, or somewhere in between. So when my brother asked me to babysit his nine-month-old son one Friday night, I agreed without hesitation.

My experience with pettable puppies and cute kitties, in my mind, put me on par with being an expert babysitter.

My brother and his wife delivered the child to my house that evening fast asleep in a charming little carrying case; it looked like a chic picnic basket with a little bitty ham inside.

SUPPER

"Two hours? A piece of cake," I assured them as they walked toward the door to leave.

Of course, it wasn't quite that simple. I had a succession of lectures from the sister-in-law about feeding, burping, diapers, rash, cream, blankets, cat hair on the floor, and the dog's tongue after he licked himself.

Thirty minutes later, I assured them that a man of my stature could handle watching my nephew.

When they had finally gone, I carefully lifted the sleeping baby from the basket and laid him on the couch. Removing his diaper with the full intent of putting on a fresh one, I grabbed a cold beer and the TV remote. I had just found my favorite show, *Cooking from the Waist Up,* when Mr. Schlitz, my cat, pounced from the back of the couch onto the kid's chest. The baby's eyes popped open like a couple of beer tabs. Spotting the cat hovering like a bad hangover, the toddler let out a scream that made the cat's hair stand on end.

I made a grab for kitty, but to no avail. A puff of air exited the youngster's lungs as the crouched cat sprang with its full weight into a nearby chair. The wails coming from that tiny body were relentless.

I yelled for Butane, my boxer, to consume the cat, but he was too busy licking his butt to be concerned.

Grabbing the infant, I cuddled him near my chest and softly patted his back. As the wailing gradually subsided, a smile eased across my face, followed by a sigh of relief. But liberation was short lived, as I felt what seemed like warm beer penetrating my shirt.

The cat had activated the kid's sprinkler system.

Holding the child at arm's length, the stream shot like a park fountain. I was in a full sprint to the kitchen to grab a clothespin when the flow suddenly subsided. I stared intently at the baby's face; he seemed at peace with himself—the well had run dry.

Gently laying the child back on the couch, I grabbed a roll of paper towels and had just finished dabbing my shirt dry when I turned to see Butane licking lovingly on the kid's face.

"Butane!" I barked. Startled, the dog crapped at the kid's feet before bolting out the doggie door.

The front door then slammed. It was my brother. "Hey, I saw your dog tearing down the road like something scared him."

My jaw dropped like a lead meatball.

"You aren't going to believe this, but we got to the show and found out our tickets aren't good until tomorrow night. How dumb is that?" he asked.

"Ye…ye…yeah, dense," I stammered. "Whe…where's Sonja?"

"She's coming. She's trying to call your dog ba—" His sentence ended like a lung had burst. "My God! What did you feed my kid?"

I was just about to explain how Butane has anxiety attacks, when his wife came through the door. Being a mother, the first thing she spotted was a pile of poo the size of ping-pong balls near her son. She let out a scream that made the cat's hair stand on end.

What followed wasn't pretty. Suffice it to say that I do have visitation rights with my nephew but that he will never again see his uncle's house without parental supervision.

Marriage? I don't think so.

Glazed Baby Carrots

My sister-in-law passed along this recipe before she decided to be a baby and not speak to me. You will need the following ingredients:

- Serves 2 (with leftovers)
- Prep time—about 5 minutes
- Cook time—about 40 minutes

2 pounds of baby carrots

1 ½ cups of water

1 tablespoon of brown sugar

> 2 tablespoons of butter
>
> ½ cup of orange juice
>
> Pour the carrots into a large skillet and add water. Cover and bring the water to a boil over high heat. Once it begins to boil, lower the heat to medium and simmer the carrots until they are tender—15 to 25 minutes, depending on their size. When tender, remove the lid, simmer, and add sugar, juice, and butter. Mix well and cook over high heat again until most of the liquid has evaporated, stirring occasionally to coat the carrots. Sweet and delicious!

Race to the Finish

Dad was a huge horseracing fan before he died. It would be more appropriate to say that he *is* a huge horseracing fan because I'm sure he's still betting on the thousands of thoroughbreds that have gone to greener pastures. And I would dare bet he's still winning.

One of the last race days that Dad and I went to was at the Finger Lakes Race Track in northwestern New York. We not only bet against the odds, we bet against each other to see who could win the most money during a day of racing. I'd like to make it clear that Dad never took advantage of anybody—not even a dumb kid who thought he could out-handicap his old man.

Following our two-hour trip to the track that bright, sunny afternoon, I sprinted to the bar and ordered a beer to kick off a day at the races. I lobbied, unsuccessfully, for Dad to have a beer as well. Never much of a drinker, he lit his pipe, tucked his racing form under his arm, and nonchalantly mentioned that the first race was only minutes away.

We purchased two box seats at the top of the grandstands and began poring over our racing forms. I quickly drained my beer and got caught up with the crowd and the smell of horse manure. "I've got my winner," I proudly exclaimed minutes later. Rising from my seat, I again filled my lungs with the distinct smells of the track. "I'm gonna grab my ticket. Are you ready?" I asked with the eagerness of a kid not yet learned in the school of life at the track.

Dad looked up, shook his head, took a puff on his pipe, and returned to studying his racing form.

Shrugging my shoulders, I pulled seven dollars from my pants pocket and swaggered to the betting window, placed my two-dollar bet, and strutted to the beer stand for a five-dollar beer.

We split the first two races; Dad won the first, me the second. When I won the second race, my confidence level soared, and I knew in my gut that I was going to outwit my dad. The horse was a long shot and paid $27.50 to win.

I had another beer, downing it with confidence.

Neither of us hit the third, and I again won the fourth. The horse paid $11.40 to win. I was in the groove. I had another beer. "Pop, you wanna sip from a winner's cup?" I asked, stumbling over my chair, spilling half my drink.

Dad smiled wryly, shook his head, and walked quietly to the ticket window.

I don't know if it was due to stupid luck that I won those two races or the consumption of alcoholic beverages that prohibited me from winning after that. But Dad won the fifth, sixth, seventh, and the eighth races; all of them. He was up nearly eight-hundred dollars.

"Do you want to play the last one?" he asked, scouring the field of horses.

I reached into empty pockets and suggested that it was a long ride home and that we should leave before the parking lot started to empty. Broke and embarrassed, I rode home munching on crow. I never again went toe-to-toe with Dad at the races. I did, however, come up with a dish I dedicated to him. It's a good one to serve to all the winners in your life.

Roy's Winner's Circle Chicken

- Serves 4
- Prep time—about 20 minutes
- Cook time—about 1 hour

4 medium-sized skinless chicken breasts

1 can condensed cream of chicken soup (10 ¾ oz.)

1 can condensed cream of mushroom soup (10 ¾ oz.)

1 can milk

Chicken seasoning

Parmesan cheese

Pour both cans of soup in a large saucepan and heat slowly. Fill one can with milk and add slowly while stirring. Once warmed through, it should turn to gravy. Heat to almost boiling and remove from hot burner. Coat a cake pan or casserole dish with cooking spray and lay chicken breasts meaty side up. Sprinkle with chicken seasoning and cheese. Next, pour the hot soup evenly over chicken. Sprinkle again with cheese. Cover and bake at 350 degrees for approximately 1 hour, or until chicken is done (no longer pink).

Calling Dr. Love

I don't know how, but I've managed to gain the reputation as a, well, for lack of a better term, *love doctor*. During a time when my life is in such a state of disarray when it comes to love and women, this term seems to me to be paradoxical. But what's a man to do? Unfortunately, I haven't found the answer to that question while this "love doctor" thing keeps snowballing.

My friend Artie may shoulder some of the blame for getting this whole thing started. Artie came to me one day last spring with a problem he was having with his girlfriend.

I've known Artie and Gertrude for seven, maybe eight years. They are, for the most part, a happy couple. But Gertrude was growing restless with the relationship. She was handing Ernie ultimatums right and left. The biggest one he brought to me.

"Look, Gertrude says that either I quit drinking, smoking, playing poker, and watching NASCAR on Sundays, or she's gonna move her mother in with us," Artie explained, his hand shaking, fumbling for a smoke.

"Holy bull!" I blurted. "What got into her?"

"I...I...I don't know," Artie stammered, scratching his balding head. "But you gotta help me. I love my Gertie. But her mother?"

"Yeah, yeah. Give me a minute," I said, pacing slowly around the room. "Okay, look, Artie, the cigarettes can probably go. They make you stink anyway. Agreed?"

"I suppose," Artie said.

"As for the rest of it, I think I have a plan that might work," I continued. "One night this week, get her drunk and suggest a game of strip poker. Strip poker never fails, especially if you play your cards right. As for NASCAR, next Sunday, just before the race begins, turn to Gertrude and shout 'Gertie, start your engine! My motor's running, and I got horsepower to spare!' She'll love you for the attention."

"Whoa...Mister, you're a genius!" Artie said, beaming, locking me in a big bear hug. I didn't again hear from Artie about his problems at home. However, he did send a guy with whom he worked to my house for a piece of advice.

"Hey, man," Roscoe began when I answered the knock at my door. "My name's Roscoe, man. I work with that Artie dude."

"Yes, I know," I said, inviting him in. "Artie said you'd be dropping by. How can I help you?"

"Lisa's like being a real freakazoid, man. Lisa's my girl. She like spasmed last night, dude, when I wanted to like, you know, have sex under the kitchen table, man. What do you think, bro? Should I dump her or ask her to have sex on top of the table?"

I stood, listening, eyebrows raised in near disbelief. It wasn't total disbelief because the guy was standing in front of me. I thought for a moment.

"Look, Roscoe, apparently Lisa feels that having sex under the kitchen table is like throwing scraps to a dog. You don't want her to feel like a dog, do you?"

"Well…"

"Roscoe!"

"Nah, man. No way. I love my little Lisa, man," Roscoe replied.

"Good, then when you go home tonight, kiss your little Lisa, tell her how much you love her, and then go have sex in the closet. She'll adore you for thinking enough of her to be naked amongst the things she loves most."

"You're the best, dude!"

Not more than a day later, I was in a grocery store buying a hambone to make soup. I had just started sorting bones in the meat section when a youthful voice came over the store's intercom: "Calling Dr. Love… Is Dr. Love in the house? Umm, I think I saw you come in. If you're here, Dr. Love, please come to the third aisle at the front checkout counter and ask for Chris." It must have been one of Roscoe's buddies. I dropped the hambones I had been fondling and walked quietly to the produce aisle. Scooping up five large lettuce leaves, I fanned them across my face and ambled to the front of the store. Depositing the leaves in a grocery cart, I left the store and drove straight to a tavern.

These are difficult times for me. Dr. Love? I can't afford that type of notoriety. I'm cooking bachelor style. That's what I do. A "Love Doctor?"

It may be time to find another shtick.

Dr. Love's Zippy Green Bean Casserole

- Serves 2 (with leftovers)
- Prep time—about 7 minutes
- Cook time—about 30 minutes

1 can (10 ¾ oz.) of cream of mushroom soup

1 can green beans (15 oz., drained)

1/2 can milk

7–8 crackers

Before you begin anything, preheat your oven at a setting of about 375 degrees. Next, heat your soup and milk over medium heat on top of the stove until hot, but not boiling, stirring occasionally. While that's heating, pour your beans into a casserole dish or meatloaf pan. When the soup is hot, not boiling but hot, take it off the stove and pour it over the beans. Crumble the crackers over the top. Bake in the oven for about half an hour, or until the crackers begin to brown.

There you have it. Makes a great, easy supper.

Ninja Chicken

As a kid growing up on the farm, we used to raise chickens for the supper table. It was routine to send one of these birds once a week to the frying pan. If you don't know much about chickens, they can be mean and nasty. You take your life into your own hands trying to catch one.

We had a big old chunk of hardwood out in the barnyard we used as a chopping block. Each week, one of us six kids would draw straws to see who would hold the chicken while Dad whacked its head off with an axe. Nobody ever wanted the short straw. It was a dirty job. But we all knew we had to eat.

We had one bird in particular that no one wanted anything to do with. She was the baddest bird on the block. We called her Bruno; not a very feminine name for a chicken, but this was no ordinary feminine bird. Bruno was a scrapper, a real barnyard fighter. We had, on numerous occasions, one-winged chickens, chickens with patches over one eye, one-toed chickens, and chickens with feathers off half their bodies—all thanks to Bruno. I was once taken to the hospital after tangling with Bruno. It was a fight I never should have pecked.

I was only nine at the time, but I hated that bird so much that occasionally after school I would hide behind the milk house and shoot corn kernels at her with my slingshot. Bruno, however, got the better of me one afternoon. I was at my usual perch behind the north wall of the milk house. It was from that angle I could view the entire barnyard where the chickens scratched for worms. Slingshot in hand, I waited...and waited...and waited. I scanned the twenty-some-odd chicken heads but didn't see Bruno's. Something wasn't right.

I no sooner rose to my feet when three white blobs splattered at my feet. Looking up, a fourth hit me square in the forehead. I cried fowl. "Bruno!" I screamed. Like a five-pound feathered ninja, Bruno, her back to the sun, leaped from her perch atop the milk house, beak open, cackling like a crazed capon, claws taking dead aim. Blinded by the light, I threw my arms up in horror. I turned to run, but Bruno landed on the back of my neck, her gnarly nails sinking an inch deep into my hide.

I dove face first into the dirt, kicking and screaming as chicken wings battered my head. Dad spotted the poultry pounding from the pantry and raced toward me with an axe. Catching a glimpse of the shiny steel glittering in the sun, I screamed again; I wasn't sure whose head he would whack. Bruno too recognized the blade. She quickly relinquished her grip and ran like a chicken into the woods.

Eventually, I recovered from the assault and had nothing but revenge on my mind. It took weeks of tactical ground maneuvers to catch the cagey bird. It was no easy task, but when I finally outfoxed her on Saturday, May 19, 1978, at 4:14 p.m., it was a day not to be forgotten. Nor was it a meal to be forgotten. I think Bruno was the best-tasting chicken I ever ate.

But with that said, this chicken ain't bad either.

I stuffed it with Bruno in mind.

Bachelor Roast Chicken

- Serves 2
- Prep time—about 25 minutes
- Cook time—about 1 to 1 ½ hours

3–3 ½ pound roasting chicken

1 box (6 oz.) chicken stuffing (top of stove kind)

3 tablespoons of butter

1 small onion (diced)

Chicken seasoning

3–4 cups water

First of all, if your chicken has a white packet stuffed inside it, take it out. Wash the chicken and place it in a roasting pan, surrender side up. Preheat the oven to 375 degrees. On top of the stove, fix the stuffing according to the directions on the box. When that's done, add the onion. Mix and stuff the bird through that big cavity between the drumsticks. Don't be afraid to pack it in tightly. You won't use all of the stuffing. Just bake the leftover in an uncovered casserole dish for about 20 minutes. It'll come in handy. Add the butter anywhere on top of the chicken. Sprinkle liberally with chicken seasoning. Add enough water to the roasting pan to cover the bottom (about 3 to 4 cups), cover with tin foil, and bake about 40 to 50 minutes. At this point, you can either fry the contents of the packet that was packed in your

> chicken, or you can feed it to the dog. It'll love you for it. Remove the tin foil after those 40 or 50 minutes are up. Baste (pour liquid over) chicken with the juices in the pan, using either a baster or tablespoon. Repeat that process every 10 minutes until the bird is golden brown.

Terry Had a Little Lamb (and Mother Cooked It)

I've prepared a lot of dishes in the past with deep-seated memories of my childhood in mind—from the bad-beaked bird we baked to future recipes you'll devour later.

But May 2006 conjured up memories of Jethro, a dearly loved pet lamb I had as a child and a friend who lives forever in my heart...and liver...and kidneys.

My parents gave me Jethro as a birthday gift at the tender age of five. Yes, Terry had a little lamb, its fleece was white as snow, and everywhere that Terry went the lamb was sure to go. He was my best bud.

Following a year of maturity, I called out to Jethro one afternoon after school, but he didn't emerge from around any corner and bound across the lush green grass as I had become accustomed to. I ran to the springhouse where he sometimes lay in the cool shade. No Jethro. I darted to the barnyard where he liked to frolic in the sun with the chickens. No Jethro. I sprinted to the milk house where he liked to sip cool milk from a metal bucket on hot summer days.

Jethro was nowhere to be found. My parents said that he ran away, went plum crazy from a wad of chewing tobacco my brother had fed him.

I was devastated.

That night at the supper table, my parents consoled me over the loss of Jethro. Mother pointed out a new dish she had fixed. She said it was duck with mustard sauce prepared just for me. We had never eaten duck before.

I stuffed myself that evening and felt better after that great cuisine. But it would be a long time before I would get over the loss of my little fuzzy friend.

I eventually moved out of the house. And after a couple of years of fostering a taste for strange recipes, I finally figured out what had happened to Jethro. It was about the time I wrote my parents this poem:

> I had my first taste of lamb at age six.
> You said it was a bird in the oven you fixed.
> At the time I didn't know we ate friends,
> But he tasted pretty good in the end.
> I'm thankful for the pet-to-pan tips,
> Ha, kitty sees me licking my lips.
>
> Long live Jethro.

Lasagna with Beef (not lamb)

- Serves 2 (or 8)
- Prep time—about 30 minutes
- Cook time—about 40 minutes

1 pound ground beef

1 28 oz. jar of spaghetti sauce

1 package (1 lb.) uncooked lasagna noodles

1 container ricotta cheese (2 lb.)

1 package shredded mozzarella cheese (8 oz.)

½ cup grated parmesan cheese

4 eggs

Brown beef in large saucepan and drain fat. Add sauce and simmer on low heat until heated through. While that's heating, cook pasta according to directions on box. When the pasta is cooked, rinse with cold water. Place a sheet of wax paper on a flat surface and lay 3 or 4 noodles on the paper. Lay another sheet of wax paper on top of noodles and repeat the process to keep noodles from sticking together. In a large mixing bowl, combine cheeses and eggs and mix well. Pour about ½ cup of sauce in an approximately 13 x 9-inch baking pan. Place about 4 lasagna noodles lengthwise over the sauce, overlapping the edges. Spread about ⅓ of the cheese mixture over pasta and cover with 1 cup of meat sauce. Repeat the layering of noodles, cheese mix, and sauce twice. Finish your masterpiece with a layer of noodles and the rest of meat sauce and top with additional Parmesan cheese. Cover with tin foil and bake at 350 degrees for about ½ hour. Remove foil and let brown—about 10 minutes. Let stand about 15–20 minutes and serve. *Side note:* you'll be eating this for a few days, or cut into single servings and freeze.

Playing Opossum—Deplorable Ploy

Red, an old friend of mine and a fellow bachelor, graciously passed along this recipe for hamburger hash. I did have to alter this recipe slightly because opossum meat isn't readily available on supermarket shelves. After all, I wanted to make this recipe as user friendly as possible. Ground beef substituted just nicely.

If you grimace at the idea of eating opossum, I must tell you that Red won the 2003 Wolverine Mountain Best Chef ribbon in the "Best Recipe for Wild Meat" category. Outside of Tennessee, however, opinions change drastically about this recipe in its purest form.

Red lives alone at the summit of Wolverine Mountain in the northwest corner of Tennessee in a tiny cabin he calls home. He lives off the land and brews his own variety of adult beverages. And he raises opossums for food.

I remember my last excursion to Wolverine Mountain to see old Red. He was occupied trying to get his two adult opossums to copulate so he'd have enough marsupial meat for the winter. Baby opossums are born thirteen days after conception, and since an average litter size is eight or nine young, Red figured he needed to have the adults mate at least three times before the first snowfall in November. Beating the first snowfall was crucial, as opossum sexual organs easily get frostbitten.

Having lived my life calculating times between sexual encounters, I did the math. It was the last part of July; the first average snowfall on Wolverine Mountain takes place around November 28. That gave the critters nearly fifty-nine days to produce three litters. Given that the female may need a couple days off between birthing sessions, I deduced that fifty-three days was plenty of time for Red to achieve his goal. "Red, fifty-three days is an eternity in bachelor-speak," I said jokingly.

"You don't understand," Red replied, prodding the male opossum with a stick. "Watch what happens when he gets near her. She acts just like Doris used to." Doris was the woman Red almost married.

I understood better when the male approached its mate. She first hissed and then bared her teeth as if ready to rip off an organ. When his advances continued, the female fell into a catatonic state, fell on her side, and appeared dead. "See! See!" Red exclaimed, pointing the stick at the female. "Just like Doris! She'd do that every time I set foot in the bedroom. And look at that poor bastard," he said, pointing to the male. "He just lumbers away like I used to do."

I felt bad for Red. I felt even worse for the male opossum. "Red, I'd be going nuts if I was that poor critter," I said, kicking at the dirt.

"Oh, she'll come around," he answered, breaking the stick in two over his knee. "It just rattles me to no end how much she reminds me of Doris when she'd play 'possum."

I awoke the following morning before sunrise to pack. I wanted to get off that mountain before again witnessing that opossum playing opossum. Being a bachelor's tough enough. To watch a critter driven to dejection was just more than I could bear to see again.

Ladies, should you stumble upon this recipe, remember that playing 'possum hurts the one who loves you.

Hamburger Hash

- Serves 2 (with leftovers)
- Prep time—about 20 minutes
- Cook time—about 30 minutes

2 medium potatoes (peeled and diced)

2 cups of frozen peas

1 medium onion (chopped)

1 pound of ground beef

1 clove of garlic (peeled, chopped), or you can buy minced garlic in a jar

Olive oil

Chicken seasoning (optional)

Salt and pepper

Dice potatoes into small cubes by standing the potato on its end and cutting in half. Lay flat and cut each half down the middle again. Cut each section crosswise into ½ inch cubes. Dice your onion much the same way. Chop the garlic clove into small pieces. In a nonstick frying pan, add enough olive oil to cover the bottom of the pan. Add potatoes, onion, and garlic and cook until potatoes are tender and browned. In a separate frying pan, brown the ground beef and drain. Very important: if you don't have another frying pan, transfer the cooked potatoes to a bowl and cook the ground beef. The two must be cooked separately. When both are cooked, mix together, add peas and salt and pepper to taste, sprinkle with chicken seasoning, and simmer on low heat for about 10 minutes to allow the flavors to blend.

Cooking from the Garden of Good and Spooky

The only disadvantage I've found to being a bachelor is the occasional "dry spell." A dry spell is that sporadic period of time when a compatible woman is about as hard to find as a chickpea in a pail of pink paint.

One such spell happened during October 1999. Halloween Eve was at hand. Nightmares had been occurring regularly as the loneliness and desperation for companionship had me in its shroud. It was the first Halloween I'd be spending alone, instead of preparing a monster meal to share with a woman.

That October night was a particularly warm evening, and an owl's question of "Who? Who?" resonated in the heavens as the rustling of dry, crusted leaves swirled eerily in the wind outside my bedroom window. The setting fit both my mood and the night.

Turning out the light, I was soon dead to the world.

I was startled awake in the deep hours of darkness by the sound of a woman crying. I thought it was an episode from my dream, in which I had burned the sweet potatoes my date had so anxiously awaited. But I soon realized the sobbing was coming from the garden.

Donned in white-checkered boxers and a pair of blue sneakers, I walked cautiously across the backyard. In the pale light of the moon, I saw her sitting on a large orange pumpkin amidst rows of dried-out corn stalks and ripe zucchini, head in hands, weeping. She was wearing black knee-high boots, black shorts, and a black halter top. Although I wondered what she was doing in my garden, the questions stopped there.

I laid a warm hand upon her cold shoulder and asked if she would like to come inside for a glass of soothing wine and a bowl of garden-fresh Brussels sprouts. She looked up at me, eyes as dark as the night, brushed away a tear, and took my hand. We walked to the house without a word between us.

The occurrence was a dream come true—in the final hours, a woman to share my Halloween Eve.

The last thing I remember was going to bed, once again hearing the owl's question of "Who? Who?" as it resonated in the heavens and the rustling of dry, crusted leaves as they swirled eerily in the wind outside my bedroom window.

But peace was not to be mine. To my horror, I awoke at daybreak beside a large orange pumpkin, hugging two dried-out corn stalks, and kissing a zucchini.

I can't even get a dream right.

Zucchini Boats

- Serves 4
- Prep time—about 20 minutes
- Cook time—about 1 hour

1 medium-sized zucchini

1 pound ground beef

1 egg

10 saltine crackers (crushed)

1 package shredded Mozzarella cheese (8 oz.)

Ketchup

Worchester sauce

Garlic salt

Cut the ends off the zucchini and split lengthwise. Scrape out the center fleshy part of the zucchini in each half, leaving approximately ½ inch on the bottom and sides. Place both halves in a large casserole dish. In a bowl, combine ground beef, egg, crackers, about 6 shakes of Worchester sauce, and a sprinkling of garlic salt. Stir until well mixed. With a spoon or fork, pack each zucchini half with the mixture until it's about even with the top. Add 1 cup of water to the dish. Drizzle ketchup across the top of both "boats." Cover and bake at 375 degrees for about 1 hour. During the last 5 minutes of cooking, uncover and top with cheese. When cheese is melted, you're ready to cruise.

Love in a Bucket

I acquired the following recipe while dating Dominique, a woman I met in France. The turnover filling is slightly altered because in France they sauté snails and use the resulting gravy to fill their crusts.

I'm not yet to the point of swallowing snails.

Dominique invited me to participate in the process of collecting the highly prized snails used in this dish, a practice most French keep secret. It was a warm spring evening, just before sunset. Dominique handed me a small metal bucket and a chunk of moldy cheese and told me to "polish" the inside of the pail.

"Snails don't like cheese," she said. "They won't try to run if you rub it with cheese."

I nodded, eyes watering, understanding why snails retreated from the stinky stuff. I scrubbed the inside of the pail with the cheese all the while wondering how snails would have time to crawl out of a bucket. Snails are snails. They only have one gear. But I never questioned Dominique. She had me on a string.

When I finished with the cheese rub, Dominique took my hand and led me to a small patch of woods just behind her house.

"There," she said, pointing to a rotted log. "There you will find snails."

I put the pail on the ground and slowly overturned the dead wood; sure enough, two snails the size of ping-pong balls. I picked them up and put them in the pail. (I swear I heard them choke from cheese fumes.) We continued our search, overturning logs until we collected enough for our meal.

During our hunt, the sun had slowly slipped behind the trees. As darkness hovered, it soon became apparent why we needed the cheese bucket. A practiced lover, Dominique deftly opened the buttons on my shirt. With a whisper that could have melted an ice block, she breathed in my ear, "Always wait until it is night before saying that it has been a fine day."

I dropped my snail pail. We had not been this far before. The French connection that followed was nothing short of fine. Nearly an hour had passed when Dominique helped me from the forest floor. My head reeling, knees knocking, I peeked into the pail. We had lost not a single snail.

Back inside the house, Dominique rummaged through the cupboards for the cooking utensils we needed. Singing like a schoolgirl, I carried the wheezing snails to the sink and washed the rotted wood and dirt from their shells.

I couldn't watch as Dominique dropped the little guys into about half an inch of scalding water. I'm sympathetic toward creatures with shells dropped into boiling water. I once heard a lobster scream, "Not me!" when I dropped him in a pot of boiling water. Scarred me for life; although I'm certain these guys were pretty much out of it from inhaling the cheese vapors.

Once cooked, we cracked the snail shells, scraped them clean, and added the meat to a small frying pan. Dominique mixed a little flour to the water they had simmered in and made a thick gravy. She added that to the meat in the frying pan and mixed it well. Dominique then filled two pastry shells with the mixture and baked the whole kit and caboodle.

I was hesitant about eating snails. After all, I had rescued those little guys from under a dark, cold, rotted log, bathed and dried them, and provided a reunion of sorts on a large kitchen platter. However, after a little urging from Dominique, I finally gave in. I ate at a snail's pace but actually enjoyed it. The dish tasted like chicken.

You won't have to go through nearly as much trouble, but you will enjoy this version of a French dish just as much.

Ham and Broccoli Turnover

- Serves 2 (with leftovers)
- Prep time—about 15 minutes
- Cook time—about 30 minutes

Two prepared pie crusts

1 package frozen chopped broccoli

½ pound ham (slices are easier)

1 package of any shredded cheese (8 oz.)

1 package country-style gravy (1.25 oz.)

To make this dish, you'll need two cookie sheets. I suggest making both pie crusts because I know the life of a bachelor and what'll happen to any unused portions of food. Besides, you can freeze what you don't eat for a night where you're really pressed for something to eat. Unroll pie crusts and let stand. Cook broccoli according to package and drain. Cut ham into bite-sized chunks. Cook gravy mix according to package. Or you can use a gravy mix that comes in a jar. When everything is cooked and cut, fill one of the shells with about two or three tablespoons of broccoli. Make a line right down the center of the shell. Add the same amount of ham in the same manner, and the same with the gravy, being sure to spoon it so you cover the ham and broccoli. Sprinkle with cheese, as much as you like, and fold the crust over the ingredients. Press the edges of the dough together with a wet fork to seal everything inside. Poke a few holes in the crust with a fork or toothpick and bake at 400 degrees for approximately 30 minutes, or until crust is browned.

No French chef needed here!

"Tanked" Giving, Pilgrim Style

If you're a Thanksgiving traditionalist, you may want to read some other story because what I'm about to relate is gonna blow another hole in your turkey.

According to the literature *I've* read, the original so-called "Thanksgiving" was more of a drunken free-for-all than a giving of thanks for a bountiful food harvest.

The story began when the pilgrims set ground at Plymouth Rock on December 11, 1620. The snow was deep, the howling winds bitter cold. The new arrivals made the *Mayflower* their home for the remainder of the winter, drinking rum and exhausting their supplies of barreled flour and dill pickles.

By the time spring sprang, the party from England had befriended Massasoit and his Indian tribe. Massasoit was the chief of Plymouth Rock, and since meeting the pilgrims he had acquired a taste for English rum. In exchange for the liquor, Massasoit traded venison, turkey wings, and burnt pumpkin seeds.

As the days grew longer and warmer, the Indians and the pilgrims became inseparable. They held barrel races and played "Pin the Flag on the Totem Pole." Each learned the other's language and dating practices. There was so much harmony, in fact, that the two groups formed a band. They called themselves the Village People. Massasoit hammered on the drums, Squanto sang bass, and Pocahontas sang tenor. Other band members included Miles Standish on screaming guitar, John Smith, "the fiddlin' fool," and William Bradford, who set the piano ivories on fire.

As that summer drew to an end and the land exploded in a lightshow of red, gold, and orange, the Village People wanted to throw a party. The event had nothing to do with a bountiful harvest but rather the arrival of a Greek ship that had docked at Plymouth Rock while on its way to Cuba. The floating crate was chock-full of the finest wine Greece had to offer. Both Standish and Smith were very fond of the grape. And soon, so too were the Indians. Everyone now had a reason to throw a bash, and food wasn't it.

The Village People billed the event as "Howlin' at the Rock." The four-day festival featured boiled pumpkin along with lobster, clams, hickory nuts, and seaweed soup—and lots and lots of rum and wine.

So now you can dispel everything you've ever heard about the first Thanksgiving and its connotations. The day wasn't a giving of thanks but rather a full-blown rowdy rock 'n roll event that had the Pilgrims and the Indians gettin' down in Massachusetts.

And you read it here first.

Lobster and Clam Thanksgiving

- Serves 1
- Prep time—none
- Cook time—according to lobster size (see below)

1 (or 2) 1 ½-pound fresh lobster

1 dozen little neck clams

½ stick of butter

Now here's a real bachelor's Thanksgiving meal. No fuss, no muss. And it's sure to impress your company. (I hope you have company.) Begin by filling a large pot with water (enough to cover lobsters). Bring water to full boil and add one tablespoon of salt per quart of water. Put the lobsters in claws first and begin timing from the moment the water comes back to a boil. When done, simply peel and eat!

For 1 pound: 5 minutes

1 ¼ pounds: 8 minutes

1 ½ to 2 pounds: 8 to 10 minutes

For the clams, simply put them on a plate, slide them into the microwave, and cook until the shells pop open. The water inside the clams naturally steams them. It's that easy!

Of course, enjoy both the lobster and the clams dipped in melted butter.

What Sex on the Beach?

They say that age is but a number. I used to believe it myself. However, as the numbers add up, I now believe that philosophy to be flawed.

I can't really pinpoint when my attitude began to change, but I can share by example.

Without creating prejudice by giving specific numbers pertaining to my age, I'll just say that it began a few years ago while vacationing at the New Jersey shore. The day was gorgeous, the sky a carpet of blue. My attention was centered on a young woman walking along the boardwalk. She was a beautiful brunette, tanned to perfection, wearing a black halter top and a snow-white towel wrapped tightly around her waist. She had the air of a model on a runway. She was stunning. I grabbed my binoculars to focus more precisely on her movements.

"Like what you see?"

Somewhat startled, I turned to see a gentleman about my age standing resolutely in the sand directly behind me. He had in his hand a rolled-up newspaper; a pair of binoculars dangled from his neck.

"Oh, man, grab your glasses! You have to check this out!" I exclaimed, turning, pointing excitedly toward the young woman.

I no sooner got the words out of my mouth when the man cracked me on the right side of my head with the newspaper. "That's my twenty-year-old daughter, you pervert!" he shouted as he continued his paper assault.

I struggled to gather my belongings.

"Look, I just—"

Crack!

"I didn't mean—"

Crack!

I dropped face first into the beach, frantically trying to cover my head.

Relentlessly pummeled until sand packed both nostrils and one ear, I began gasping for breath. The irate dad took a respite from his beating. Rising quickly to my knees, I desperately wiped away half the coastline from my tongue with one hand as I dug furiously with a finger from the other into my left nostril to clear an airway.

Another crack from the newspaper cleared the right nostril.

"Now wait a minute!" I cried.

"That's my daughter!" the guy shouted.

"I know! No, wait, I didn't know!" I screamed. "I was just watching a babe on the boardwalk! No, I was watching your daugh—no, I was watching a woman! Hey, I don't know what I was doing!"

I was just about to cover my head in anticipation of another assault when the young woman I was watching strolled up to her father.

"Dad, is this poor old man okay? Are you trying to help him?"

Her words echoed in my head like the desolate sea in a time-worn shell washed ashore.

"No, no, he's not," the father replied. "Let's go find your mother."

"But aren't you going to help him, Dad?" the daughter asked.

"I did," he replied sternly.

As the two walked down the beach, I dug a hole in the sand and buried my binoculars.

I'm currently in talks with my travel agent for a trip to Antarctica for next year's vacation.

To bring land and sea together without the threat of being thumped, whoop up this chicken and seafood dish. It's quick, easy, and absolutely a lady pleaser.

Chicken/Seafood Pasta

- Serves 2
- Prep time—about 10 minutes
- Cook time—about 30 minutes

1 cup imitation crabmeat or lobster meat

1 cup cut up cooked chicken

½ cup diced green pepper

2 tablespoons of butter

½ box (16 oz.) angel hair pasta

1 (1.25 oz. packet) country-style gravy mix

Garlic salt

Cook the pasta according to box directions. Rinse and set aside. Melt your butter over medium heat in a medium- to large-sized frying pan. When it's melted, add your crabmeat, chicken, and green pepper. Sautee (cook, stirring occasionally) until peppers begin to soften. Probably 8–10 minutes. While that's cooking, give the mixture a couple of shakes of garlic salt if you so choose. You won't need a whole lot, just a couple of shakes. If you like garlic, give it a couple more.

In the meantime, cook your gravy mix in a small saucepan according to the directions on the packet. Watch it now. It only takes a couple of minutes. You gotta be on your toes. So easy on the alcohol if that's what you're doing. When your peppers begin to soften, turn off the heat, and you're ready to assemble. Put some pasta on a plate, top with the chicken/seafood/pepper combo, add gravy, and enjoy.

It's as easy as that.

TERRY L. MILLER

Out of Ashes, a New Bird

I've dated a lot of women in my time, searching for that special one who could, well, make me happy. The closest I came was with Tina Turnbottom. She was a kind-hearted woman, well proportioned, dark hair, olive skin. But Tina didn't know a turnip from a tomato. She couldn't even manage a manual can opener without bleeding.

On the anniversary of our first month together, Tina decided she was going to bake a meal to celebrate the occasion. I got home from work about five forty-five that evening. It was midwinter, so darkness had already settled. On the kitchen table, a cinnamon-scented candle burned brightly; an opened cold beer beckoned near a small bowl of cheese balls. In the living room, a melody of saxophones and bass filled the air. Tina emerged from the pantry, barefoot, carrying a can of corn, wearing the nightgown I'd gotten her on our second date.

"Enjoy your beer, baby," she cooed, planting a kiss on my cheek on her way to the stove. "I've got a surprise for you."

Tina turned the oven on high and sashayed to the refrigerator. Removing two chicken breasts and a box of bacon, she returned to the stove, winking as she walked by. I knew she didn't have a clue in the kitchen, but observing her sure beat watching the six o'clock news.

I sipped my beer and munched on a cheese ball as the banging of pots and pans resonated in the candlelight. Retrieving a pizza pan from the cupboard, Tina placed a layer of bacon, followed by the chicken, topped with the remaining strips of bacon, and shoved the pan into the oven.

Taking my hand, she led me into the living room where we danced lovingly in the shadows. I was on my fourth or fifth beer when a peculiar aroma crept through the darkness. Tina, thinking it was a bouquet arising from the marriage of heated chicken and pork, whispered, "Let's give it a few more minutes."

But I knew the smell of burnt animal fat. And I knew that burnt animal fat meant fire.

They say that out of the ashes rise good things. Once I had the kitchen remodeled, including a new stove, new wallpaper, floor and ceiling tile, kitchen table, and chairs, I sat one night thinking of Tina over a beer and a bowl of cheese balls. She had long since disappeared like a wisp of smoke. Her attempt at a chicken and bacon dinner, however, was seared in my mind. The following recipe is what arose from the ashes of that night.

Bacon-Wrapped Chicken on a Bed of Buttered Noodles

- Serves 2
- Prep time—about 5 minutes
- Cook time—about 1 hour

2 medium-sized boneless chicken breasts

6 strips of bacon

1 pound bag broad egg noodles

Butter

Cook half the bag of egg noodles according to directions on bag. When done, drain and set aside. Preheat oven to 375 degrees. Wrap each chicken breast with 3 strips of bacon (one on each end and one in the middle). Lay the breasts in a shallow baking dish (not a pizza pan) or casserole pan. Bake uncovered approximately 40 minutes to 1 hour, or until the chicken juices no longer are pink when poked with a fork. Bacon should be crisp but not burnt. Remove from oven and place breast on top of heated, buttered noodles. Salt and pepper to taste. You can also flavor the noodles with shredded or shaker cheese.

Fried Fish, Better Than a Stick in the Eye

With the dawn of summer, a memory of food and father sticks in my mind.

It was the same summer as my memorable lamb bake. (I'm thinking now that it was a very bad year). I was six years old, and Dad took me out one Saturday for an overnight camping trip near a fishing stream noted for plump trout that fried up to an unequaled feast on an open fire.

We made camp just before dusk that warm June night, as a pair of bullfrogs croaked their crude notes near a swamp's edge, accompanied by a chorus of peepers to create a perfect orchestra in the open night air.

Later, as the moon beamed through a canopy of trees, both of us fat from fresh trout and salt potatoes, Dad, relaxing in an old lawn chair with pipe in hand, was teaching me how to roast my first marshmallow.

"Hold it just above the tip of the flames," he said calmly, lighting his freshly filled pipe. "Now, slowly turn the stick with your fingers to let the marshmallow brown a little at a time. You got it, Son," Dad said proudly, settling in his chair, legs outstretched, warm pipe resting comfortably in hand. "Just keep turning the stick until it's browned."

A loving smile crossed my face as I turned to Dad to thank him for the trip and…

But in a flash, the calm of night erupted into mayhem. "Watch your marshmallow!" Dad barked, sitting upright in his chair. I quickly turned to see a mini fireball blazing against a backdrop of summer stars.

Jumping to my feet, I began hysterically waving the marshmallow to extinguish the flame. But the tiny inferno left my stick, shooting through the night air like a flaming orange comet. Seconds later, I heard a terrifying *splat* as Dad folded in his chair like a cheap newspaper, screaming in the mode of a horror movie star.

As he fell out of his chair and lay rolling on the ground, charred marshmallow embedded between his eyes, I danced around my floundering father, stabbing at the goo with the end of my stick in an attempt to pick it off. But Dad was rolling so fast I only managed to spear him in the left eye.

He let out another piercing scream.

Fortunately, a forest ranger heard the night howls and rushed us to a local hospital. Dad healed okay. But to this day I have a deep-seated disdain for marshmallows and their potential.

Fried Fish (Fresh or Frozen)

- Serves 2
- Prep time—about 5 minutes
- Cook time—about 8 minutes

2 fish fillets (fresh or frozen)

2 eggs

Milk

Flour

Cooking oil

Salt and pepper

There's no substitute for fresh fried fish. But if you must, a frozen fillet will suffice. Break two eggs into a small mixing bowl. Next, add a splash of milk. (Remember, a splash is tipping your milk container and counting one fishy two.) With a fork, blend the mixture until egg yolks are broken and milk and eggs are completely mixed. In a separate dish, add about a cup of flour. Now, in a large frying pan, pour enough cooking oil to cover the bottom of the pan and heat. You can tell when the oil is hot enough to fry by dipping your fork in the egg mixture and letting it drip into the hot frying pan. When the drops of egg mix sizzle, you're ready to

> fry. When ready, dip fish into the bowl of egg mix. Make sure all of the fish is covered. Remove from the bowl and allow any excess to drip away. Next, roll the fish in flour until completely covered. Carefully place in pan and fry each side until golden brown. It'll only take minutes. Salt and pepper to taste.

Outdated Date

There comes a point or two in every bachelor's life when desperation for a date drives him to do stupid things. And on that list of stupid things, just below watching Dr. Phil, is agreeing to a blind date.

My friend Bill recently divorced and, free for the better part of a year, has been doing quite well for himself. Bill's hip with the chicks while my love life is as dormant as a limbless cat. So when he asked if I wanted to double date, I figured what the heck.

I agreed to meet Bill and the two women one Saturday night at a local bar. Two margaritas, a Bud Ice, and three shots of Jack Daniels later, Bill and his entourage walked through the door. I couldn't tell which two of the babes he was with, but both were stunning. I sat straight on my barstool and slapped a respectable look on my face. Bill had come through big time—so I thought.

I watched as the bouncer stretched out his arm and asked the first woman for her driver's license. From across the room, I could hear the young lady giggle as she pulled her ID from her sock. Chewing her gum like an excited schoolgirl, she turned to her female friend and shouted, "Isn't this wild?"

Her friend, reaching into her bra to retrieve her ID, exclaimed, "Awesome!"

Bill spotted me sliding off my stool to exit out the side door. I shot him a look that he read like a book. Waving with his hand and shaking his head, he steered the girls in my direction. "Hey, hey, here we are." He pushed me back onto my stool. "Ladies, I'd like you to meet Terry."

"Hi, Terry!" they shouted in unison, sounding like a couple of high school cheerleaders. I could feel thirty-six sets of eyes straining through the smoke-filled neon lights of the bar to see who had brought their daughters out on a Saturday night.

"China, this is your date!" Bill exclaimed, quickly ordering two drinks and disappearing into the crowd.

I often marvel at the English language and the array of words that can be used to encapsulate a situation, but not this one.

"Hey, cuz," China chimed like a wind-up doll. "Wanna wipe the floor?"

Cuz? Wipe the floor? China? Somewhere between the Jack Daniels and Bud Ice, I had sipped into the Twilight Zone.

"Come on. Grab me a fruity drink and let's start hammerin,' baby!" she cooed, gyrating against the barstool.

Looking around for Bill, to choke the life out of him, I asked the bartender for a fruity drink and a double shot for me.

China was quickly on her way to Cuba as the band banged out a beat reminiscent of the Islands. Some young stud with the physique of the Total Gym salesman had pulled her to the dance floor and was grinding his body next to hers, sending her into a squealing frenzy.

I heard the bar patrons snicker as I rolled past them toward the door like the Geritol Express. The ladies at the Friday night bridge club marvel at the stories I relay to them, all but Brenda. She recommended I try the e-Harmony Web site. Stayed tuned…

If there's a blind date in your future, I suggest skipping the bar and inviting her to your place for a home-cooked meal. It might be a little difficult getting her there, but there's nothing difficult about this recipe. You'll have her coming back for seconds. I guarantee it.

Barbecue Chicken Bake

- Serves 2 (with leftovers)
- Prep time—about 20 minutes
- Cook time—about 25 minutes

4 cups elbow macaroni

2 cups cut up leftover chicken

¼ cup barbeque sauce

1 can cream of mushroom soup

½ cup of milk

¼ cup flavored bread crumbs

Cook macaroni according to package directions. Preheat oven to 350 degrees. In a saucepan, mix chicken and barbeque sauce and heat and stir until well coated. In another saucepan, heat soup and milk; stir until smooth. Blend cooked, drained noodles with soup. Pour mixture into a casserole dish and spread evenly. Spoon chicken evenly over noodles. Top with bread crumbs. Bake for approximately 25 minutes.

The Santa Claus Shuffle

I once danced with Santa Claus. Really. It was after a cooking seminar I held for a group of bachelors at the Milk Hut Rest and Retirement Home in Lylsford, Montana.

Those guys thought themselves a bunch of studs, giddy on the idea of cooking for the widows in the building. They were like a bunch of little kids with their first Easy-Bake oven. Actually, they were more of a bunch of hooligans. Nick, the leader of the gang, was the most mischievous. He would regularly switch medicines on the boys, replacing Viagra for the other little blue pill prescriptions they took daily.

But pills weren't the only items of interest for Nick. He also liked to mix a little liquid laxative in the ladies' nighttime tea. Talk about life in the fast lane after eighty. The guys were chasing the women, the women were chasing each other to get to the bathroom, and I was chasing them all to sit down and eat before the roast beef got cold.

I was wrapping up the seminar during the third week of December 1992. The residents of the Milk Hut Rest and Retirement Home were hosting a party, and they invited me to stay.

I gladly accepted and joined the residents the night of the party. I felt honored when they told me Nick had prepared a special bowl of eggnog for me in appreciation for the seminar. I looked around to thank him but couldn't find him anywhere.

The hour soon turned to 8:30 p.m., and still no Nick. After a short evening of eating, prescriptions, and dancing the shuffle dance, the residents of the Milk Hut Rest and Retirement Home began, one by one, to shuffle off to bed. I remained behind my eggnog bowl, bursting with Christmas cheer. Not yet ready to leave, I cranked up an old Bing Crosby tune, grabbed a blow-up Santa Claus, and waltzed around the dance floor.

When I struggled to open my eyes the next afternoon under the Christmas tree, Nick and his gang stood over me with half-empty glasses of milk and cookie crumbs imbedded in the corners of their mouths.

"Look, boys, it's a pickled pixie." Nick chuckled, chugging his milk. "Did you enjoy your eggnog, Son?"

I pushed aside a deflated Santa Claus and licked a pair of parched lips, the taste of grain alcohol and vodka nauseating me when I belched. Nick handed me a little blue pill and said it would cure my hangover.

He was right. In fact, I felt better than I had in years. I was living large in the Milk Hut Rest and Retirement Home.

Nick and the boys may have been a bunch of meatballs, but they sent me home with this recipe. I was impressed and have cooked it for a couple of ladies with great success. Check it out.

Barbecued Meatball Sandwich (A Bachelor Favorite)

- Serves 2 (maybe with leftovers)
- Prep time—about 30 minutes
- Cook time—about 30 minutes

1 cup favorite beer

1 cup ketchup

¼ cup vinegar

¼ cup Worcestershire sauce

¼ cup sugar

1 pound ground beef

2 ¼ cups crushed saltine crackers

1 small onion (minced)

¼ cup mayonnaise

Hot dog or sub rolls

Combine beer, ketchup, vinegar, Worcestershire sauce, and sugar in a saucepan and mix well. Simmer over medium-low heat for about 20 minutes. In a mixing bowl, combine remaining ingredients and mix thoroughly. Shape into meatballs about the size of golf balls or smaller. Next, line a deep cereal bowl with aluminum foil, leaving about 6 inches on each end. Put half your meatballs in bowl. Pour half of the beer mixture over meatballs. With another sheet of foil, fold edges together to form a tight seal. Repeat process with remaining meatballs. Stick in fridge. Prepare charcoal or gas grill for cooking. When ready, place packets of meatballs on heat and cook approximately 20–30 minutes, turning every 5–7 minutes so they don't burn. During last 5 minutes, butter inside of rolls and place on a sheet of foil over heat until browned. You better have your honey over for this one!

Real Men, Where Are You?

The bachelor strain of real men I have come to know and admire in my lifetime seems to be disappearing. And it alarms me. I arrived at this conclusion after a web search on "bachelors" to determine how others in my genre are faring in their pursuit of the perfect woman.

The results were not pretty.

I began with the phrase "bachelor life." The first site I perused was maintained by a lonely guy living in England, whose concerns were in this order: a 3-D TV, a smaller laptop, an iPod phone, and the "reality of sitting home alone." What is that? Talk about out-of-whack priorities. Little wonder he's sitting at home bemoaning the fact that he's sitting at home alone. I'm surprised he didn't mention his underwear was too tight.

I tried a different site. This guy's most recent blog had him lamenting about a full bag of potatoes and fruit flies. Grasp the picture. A single guy whining about potatoes and fruit flies. He went on to talk about broccoli sprouting arms and legs and somehow jumping from his refrigerator when he went to grab a yogurt cup. Fruit flies or fruitcake? I shook my head in dismay.

Hesitantly, I pointed my arrow and clicked another so-called bachelor site.

This blog began praising toilet paper. Peter P. wrote about "crumpling the paper so it's softer." He shared his insights on how "two sheets of toilet paper can be folded to make a comfortable pad, to reduce waste, for the environmental conscious in all of us." I was so stewed that I ran to the bathroom and counted out fifty-two sheets of Charmin and flushed them.

Is this what bachelors are talking about these days? Smaller laptops, potatoes, fruit flies, and toilet paper? Whatever happened to the good old days of wine and women and satin sheets? It used to be when men were men, women followed. What I'm reading on the blogs today boils down to nothing short of the feminization of our male culture. And it's pretty disconcerting.

Don't read me wrong. I love women. But when a guy starts singing the praises of toilet paper, something in America has gone awry—the chickification of the male species. I lost sleep for two consecutive nights over this phenomenon. When I again returned to the computer, I did a keyword search of "real men." Again, I was astounded.

Sal W., in Tinworths, Utah, devoted an entire blog to "How Real Men Have a Dialogue with the Opposite Sex." I read it with amazement. Gone were the sexy pickup-lines of yesterday, including some of my favorites:

"Mmm...your hair smells like doughnuts."

"I'm just gonna skip the corny pickup line and get straight to the part where you slap me."

"If I were coffee, you would be my Coffee-mate."

"The little people behind my eyes that yell at my brain told me to tell you just how sexy you are."

My most successful line ever, "Hey, baby, were you born in a brewery? 'Cause I'd sure like to pop your top."

This guy was definitely in touch with his feminine side, offering a platitude of touchy-feely words like *soft, sensitivity,* and *subtle*. I wanted to puke.

Maybe Sal should have been named Sally.

Then a Web site jumped from the screen—Nine-Inch Male Pump Action 243. Finally! The screen name screamed masculinity. I pointed my mouse with abandon and clicked.

"Yoo-hoo...come on guys and gals. I'm still searching for those nine-inch pink pumps I saw posted on Rita's blog. What are you waiting for? Please write to me and tell me where I can find them..."

The doctor said my prescription cannot be refilled.

But the Internet is not without its rewards. A fellow bachelor sent to my blog this casserole dish that had me believing once again that real men do exist.

Tater Tot Casserole

- Serves 4
- Prep time—about 20 minutes
- Cook time—about 1 ½ hours

1 ½ pound ground beef

¼ cup of ketchup

¼ cup milk

1 onion chopped

1 ½ slices of bread (broken up)

1 egg

2 cans of cream of mushroom soup (10.75 oz.)

1 package of shredded cheese (8 oz. of your favorite)

1 package of frozen tater tots

To begin, preheat your oven to 400 degrees. Next, add ground beef, ketchup, milk, onion, bread, and egg to a large mixing bowl. With a wooden spoon, or with your hands, thoroughly mix the ingredients. Add mixture to a medium-sized, square casserole dish and flatten out evenly to each corner of the dish. Add both cans of soup and spread evenly. Sprinkle cheese evenly over top of the soup. Then add a single layer of tater tots to cover the entire dish. Bake for about 1–1 ½ hours, or until meat is cooked and no longer pink and tots are golden brown.

Pasta Overload

I was recently invited to a pasta buffet by someone I'd never met. Adrianne claimed to be a devout reader of my words. She said it had become hard for her to find a date. She wondered if, since I seemed to have such a hard time finding a date, I would accompany her to the noodle extravaganza.

The invitation caused me to reflect on dates and relationships.

I once dated an Italian girl, Ruth, which turned out to be one of the most bloated relationships I've ever been in.

Ruth was raised to love brother, sister, mother, father, and food; pasta, to be precise. Ruth loved egg noodles with butter in the morning, ravioli in the afternoon, and baked ziti for supper. On Tuesdays and Thursdays, however, she'd spice it up and have rigatoni with ham bits for breakfast, manicotti for lunch, and sausage and shells for supper.

When I met Ruth, she was twenty-three, petite, and knock-out-lift-you-up-lay-you-down-and-leave-you-gasping gorgeous. I never thought twice about her eating pasta at every sitting meal. After all, when a bachelor meets a woman who stands five-foot-four, weighs ninety-seven pounds, whose face is etched with goddess features, whispers with the voice of an angel, and possesses eyes and hair mirroring the darkest night you could imagine, her eating habits are the last thing that spur him.

I was in love. I was so much in love that I asked Ruth to move in with me. We had a whirlwind romance that took us both to heights neither of us had ever dreamed possible. We shared endless manicotti, rigatoni, and tortellini.

But our bond soon collapsed like a stuffed shell void of filling.

Now that I think back, there were a few things I could have done to save the relationship. Well, make that one—pasta psychotherapy. Someone needed to get inside her "noodle."

Six months into our dating, I began to notice her carbohydrate count climb. Her cheeks became more round, resembling a chipmunk packing nuts. Her voice grew deeper, comparable to a mama cow bellowing for its calf. And her body expanded like an air mattress slowly pumped full of air.

I tried to warn Ruth of impending peril. But she wouldn't listen. The addiction to carbohydrates was too tough, the need for noodles too strong. Ruth delved deeper and deeper into the carbo caverns of hell. I repeatedly ventured into those caverns to try to rescue her through offerings of passion fruits and voluptuous vegetables. But my efforts fell on tasteless tongue.

The relationship abruptly ended the night she came home with a large meat-lovers pizza in her left hand, a half-eaten stromboli in her right, and a canoli dangling from her lips like an albino cigar. She looked like a parade float advertising an all-you-can-eat buffet.

So, Adrianne, I must decline your invitation. My life as a misguided bachelor will continue until the day comes when I have *my* noodle examined and the memories of albino cigars and bloated love exist no more. Until then, eat hearty. Enjoy the endless pasta buffet. Fill your plate with fedelini, fettuccine, and fusilli.

I'll be watching the parade.

Steak and Spaghetti

- Serves 2
- Prep time—none
- Cook time—about 20 minutes

2 tablespoons of butter

2 tablespoons of minced garlic

½ package of spaghetti

1 medium-sized tenderloin steak

Cook spaghetti according to directions on the box. While the spaghetti is cooking, melt butter over low heat and add garlic. Let simmer while you cook your steak, watching so that it doesn't burn. To cook steak, place on foil-lined cookie sheet and broil approximately 4 minutes per side. When meat is cooked, cut into bite-sized pieces. When spaghetti is done, drain but don't rinse. Return to hot pot. Add melted garlic butter and toss. Add cut steak. Toss. Enjoy.

APPETIZERS

Over the Ocean Blue... or Black

Here's a little-known fact: when Columbus first landed on America's east side, his ship was carrying forty crates of prized English-bred chickens. Chris had made a deal with the Queen of England. He told the queen that if he was right in his assumption that the world was round and not flat, as she had suspected, that he and his crew would need at least four hundred chickens to stay healthy, procreate, and establish a new colony so she could cruise across "the Big Pond," take a little vacation, maybe build a summer home, and return to England, assured that her money that sponsored his voyage had been well spent and that she could prosper in the new territory.

The queen, high on the idea of having a vacation home in a foreign land, accepted Chris's proposal.

All was well with the arrangement until the Native Americans caught wind of Chris's deal and cried foul. Knowing the chaos the coming of a queen could bring, the Indians, in turn, conspired to pluck Columbus of his chickens and send him packing.

Late one night, while sitting around a campfire, Chief Holy Buzz passed a peace pipe filled with some "smoke" his friends from Mexico had taught him to cultivate. Chris, never having partaken of the pipe before, became extremely lightheaded and happy. Throwing his arms around his newfound smoking buddy, giggling wildly, Chris traded the four hundred chickens for a couple ounces of the homegrown weed.

Chris and his crew, like a bunch of school kids, smoked their booty in a few short days. With no chickens to slaughter and desperate for food and munchies, the men began stealing from the Indians. With each visit to the village, the men stuffed ears of corn in their pants and rolled-up venison jerky in their shirtsleeves. But the Indians caught on quickly to what was happening, especially when the village women began noticing the white men walking around looking like porn stars.

When Chief Holy Buzz confronted Columbus concerning the thievery, Chris profusely apologized and blamed the ill behavior of him and his men on global warming. The chief, all the wiser, accepted the explorer's explanation in part to save any possible tribal fallout from those in the clan who also believed environmental change was occurring.

Punishment had to be dealt swiftly, however, to quell the situation. The chief, trying to save face and ward off future shenanigans by the white men and an uprising by his own people, banished Chris and his crew to their boats, instructing them never to set foot in the territory again.

It's not clear how Columbus and his crew managed to survive without the help of the Indians. Some believe they sailed farther south and secured the aid of a Mexican drug cartel in northern Florida.

In the months that followed, Chief Holy Buzz found ways to cook chicken like the entire Indian nation had never seen before—including this recipe that was discovered rolled up in paper that looked amazingly like a cigarette.

Go figure.

Chicken Fingers

- Serves 2
- Prep time—about 15 minutes
- Cook time—about 20 minutes

2 boneless chicken breast halves

2 cups crushed cracker crumbs

1 egg (beaten)

Garlic powder

Salt

Chili powder

Wash chicken breasts and cut into strips approximately 1 inch wide. Mix cracker crumbs and seasonings to taste. If you like spicy "fingers," add approximately half a teaspoon of chili powder and garlic powder to cracker crumbs. If you don't like it so spicy, add less. This is your call. When you have your cracker crumbs and seasoning mixed, dip chicken pieces into egg mixture and coat with cracker-crumb mixture. Put chicken pieces on cookie sheet sprayed with cooking oil. Bake at 375 degrees for 15–20 minutes, or until browned. Serve with ketchup, mustard, or your favorite sauce.

Philosophy 101 Minus Eleven

As I sat drinking lunch in a saloon on the outskirts of Dakarta, South Dakota, I pondered how my life had taken the turn that it had involving women. Decades had passed since puberty, and here I sat with whispers of wrinkles and an all-out assault against the gray that defined older men. I stared at a framed picture of a young buxom blonde that hung above the Jack Daniels and Tanqueray bottles on the saloon shelves and thought about my high school and college years. Every friend I made in my early years either had sons or daughters headed off to college, or were making their last child support payments.

I was biting the last half of a deep-fried corn ball when an attractive younger-than-middle-aged woman sat on the barstool beside me. She pulled a Parliament cigarette from her pack but buried her head in her hands before lighting it. "Why me," she quietly moaned. "Why does it always happen to me?"

Swallowing the last of the corn ball crust, I ordered a beer and turned to the woman beside me. "Can I buy you a drink, Michelle?"

In a full body spasm, the woman in succession broke her unlit cigarette, choked on air, and knocked her stool over, backpedaling toward the door. "How did you know my name?" she demanded, pulling a can of pepper spray from her purse.

"Whoa." I smiled, raising my glass. "It's on your shirt."

Glancing at her left breast, Michelle wept loudly. She picked up her stool and again sat down beside me. Burying her head in hands, she again blubbered, "Why me? Why does this always happen to me?"

Now, being educated and vulnerable, I could spot vulnerability. Finally there was someone harboring as much misery as me. I indiscreetly wiped the corn ball crumbs and beer foam from the corners of my mouth. Closing my eyes, I hurled a Hail Mary in desperation. "Look, Michelle, I'm staying at the Hampton Inn over on 86 if you'd like to come over and talk about it."

The woman raised her head, looked me square in the eye, and in a dead tone of voice replied, "I want an ugly man."

"I'm sorry, what did you say?" I asked, baffled.

"I want an ugly man," she reiterated. "An ugly man would adore me."

A nearly burnt bulb flickered in my head. I had often witnessed ugly guys in the company of gorgeous women, no different than the beautiful woman beside me, and wondered what those fortunate guys possessed that I didn't. This woman was revealing the mystery—I was too good looking! I sat for a moment, dumbfounded by the revelation. All my life I had convinced myself that I possessed the ugly duckling syndrome—that indeed I could not attract an attractive mate because I looked more like a mudslide than a daiquiri; not the fact that I was too good looking. I felt good and depressed at the same time. Here sat a beautiful young woman about to get loaded in the middle of the afternoon in a small town in South Dakota, and I didn't have a shot with her because I was too good looking.

I had to think fast.

"Look, Michelle, I'm not really good looking," I said, trying to pull thoughts out of my butt faster than a tick-infested chimpanzee. "In fact, I'm pretty hideous. And even if you think I am good looking, you'd be wrong. In a scientific survey done in Tanzania in the early 1940s, it was determined that what women see on the outside of a man is opposite of what that man really appears."

I had her attention. Ordering two shots of Jack Daniels, I continued, clueless of where I was going.

"The physical makeup of a man, Michelle, is an illusion brought on by two things: one, the time of day in which the said man is being viewed. Secondly, the emotional state of the viewer upon the said subject is directly influenced by the sub-fetal area of the brain that determines cause and effect."

I ordered two more shots as Michelle puffed away on her Parliament. We touched glasses and downed our booze. I looked at my watch.

"It's now just past noon," I continued. "Because of the kinetic energy brought on by the movement of the sun, you see me in a different light. And that correlates in no indirect way with your emotional state. Now, when you factor these two phenomena together, what you really see before you is one ugly, pathetic individual disguised as a good-looking man."

Michelle held my face in her delicate hands and looked deep into my eyes. Planting a kiss squarely on my lips, she whispered, "Thank you."

I couldn't believe it. I did it! Reaching into her pocketbook, Michelle retrieved her cell phone and hit autodial. I thought she must be calling work to tell them she wouldn't be in for the rest of the afternoon. I slid the bartender a twenty-dollar tip and winked. "Lucky day for both of us," I murmured with a grin.

But my jubilation quickly turned to desolation as my cosmic stars aligned.

"Hi, Elliot. Honey, I'm sorry. Baby, I was so wrong. Can you meet me at your apartment?"

The bartender winked as he tucked the twenty-dollar bill into his shirt pocket. "At least one of us got lucky," he said with a smile.

As I drove out of Dakarta heading south, I closed another chapter in my pathetic life and entertained thoughts of opening another. Storey County, Nevada, is home to one of most infamous pieces of real estate in the country. They call the spread the Mustang Ranch. And from what I hear, I can almost be excited.

And you can be excited about these fried oysters. Whether you're having the boys over for poker or football, or a favorite female over for dinner, these make great appetizers.

Fried Oysters

- Serves 2
- Prep time—about 10 minutes
- Cook time—about 2 minutes

1 pint oysters, rinsed and drained

1 cup cornmeal

1 cup all-purpose flour

6–8 cups vegetable oil

Red pepper flakes and salt to taste

Mix flour and cornmeal evenly. Place drained oysters in large bowl and sprinkle with red pepper flakes and salt and set aside. Heat oil in large pot or deep fryer to 375 degrees. When the oil is hot, roll oysters in flour/cornmeal mixture. Fry oysters until golden brown (about 2 minutes).

Hold the Bacon, Please!

A thoughtful lady e-mailed me saying how she laughed when reading about bachelorhood. She quickly added, however, how she cried when she perused the cholesterol-laden recipes accompanying the articles. I take all my e-mail seriously. Her words, combined with the warnings my doctor has been giving me, the overlap when I tighten my belt, and the trash bag full of beer cans began to mesh.

I made a declaration designed around a note from cyberspace.

It so happened that April was also my turn to host the weekly card game with the boys. We meet (or met) every Friday night to play Slap Jack and talk guy stuff.

Benny, Roger, and Sid came to the game hungry and thirsty as usual. As they sat around the card table, they swapped stories about their wives' antics during the week.

"Bring on the brew and let's get started," Benny belted. "It's been a long week talking with our wives," he added as the guys all cheered.

I withdrew to the kitchen and returned with a tray holding four full glasses, humbly placing one in front of each of the guys.

"Hey, where's the beer?" Lenny asked, inspecting his glass full of liquid in the light.

"Gentlemen, tonight the name of the game is heart smart," I replied. "I've been enlightened. Cheers," I said, raising my glass.

Sid was the first to sip and spit.

"What is that?" he exclaimed.

"Cranberry juice with a hint of lemon and a little twist of lime. It's heart healthy," I said cheerfully.

"Come on." Peter puckered. "Where's the beer?"

"I...I don't have any."

"Bring on the wings then and cut the crap," Benny bellowed, shoving his glass aside; it was ceremonial to have chicken wings with our beer. I wiped a wee bead of sweat from my brow.

Again returning from the kitchen, I placed a platter before my guests.

"Toothpicks?" Sid said. "You're serving food with toothpicks? Where are the wings?"

"Guys, trust me. You're gonna love this," I said with a hapless grin.

Benny bit first and went ballistic.

"They're tofu bites," I shouted, "with a low-fat mayonnaise dipping sauce!"

"Are you off your rocker?" Roger ranted.

"You trying to kill us?" Benny barked.

Sid sat stunned.

One by one, the guys pushed their chairs from the table, each dropping a tofu bite into their cranberry juice as they left.

I haven't been invited to a game since.

As for the thoughtful lady who e-mailed me—well, this recipe's for her.

I hope she has a tissue.

Seafood Snackers

- Serves 4–8
- Prep time—about 20 minutes
- Cook time—about 25 minutes

1 pound imitation seafood

1 pound of bacon

These simple little snackers are great for your next card game (if you're lucky enough to be invited to one). There are a few varieties of imitation seafood, so check the package carefully. The kind you want for this recipe look like seafood sticks. If your market doesn't have this kind, the chunky kind will work too. If using the sticks, simply cut into 2- or 3-inch pieces. With a sharp knife, cut the entire pound of bacon strips in half (it's much easier than cutting a single piece of raw bacon). Next, wrap a half bacon strip around your seafood. Wrap it so the ends of the bacon rest underneath your seafood; that'll keep it from unfolding while it cooks. If using the chunky seafood, the same process works. Wrap as many as you want and place on an ungreased cookie pan. Place in oven and bake at 375 until bacon is fully cooked but not crispy—20 to 30 minutes. Since oven temperatures vary, once the cooking process begins, watch closely so the bacon doesn't burn!

The Cereal Lady Killer

When I swore off trying to find a good woman at poker games, I decided to do the one thing that finally made sense to me—I began watching Oprah.

Oprah knows women. And the more I watched, the more I learned. In fact, I learned that one of the best places to meet women is in the supermarket. Oprah also educated me on the fact that women love puppies and cute little kids. Not owning a puppy, I presented myself at my neighbor's door.

"Hi, Marge. I was wondering if I could take little Timmy to the grocery store?"

Marge shot me an odd look. I explained to her that I was writing a book and needed to perceive a grocery store through the eyes of a child. After a series of exchanges, Marge finally put on little Timmy's shoes and sent us on our way.

Timmy was only four, but I explained to him what my mission was and why I brought him along. Nodding his head all the way into the store, he really seemed to understand.

"How about that one!" Timmy suddenly shouted as we entered the store, pointing to the produce aisle.

The boy was gifted. The lady was stunning. I tucked Timmy behind me and walked up to the woman to make polite conversation. She was holding a cantaloupe and a piece of kiwi fruit.

"Say, that sure is a beautiful melon," I said, admiring the cantaloupe.

I never saw the kiwi coming.

Picking pieces of the fruit from my ear, I muttered, "What a frosted flake." Then it hit me—the cereal aisle. The cereal aisle would be a wonderful place to find a lucky charm. And I was right; the moment I turned the corner to the cereal section, I saw a special Kay. Well, she looked liked a Kay anyway, with her glasses pulled to the end of her nose, reading a cereal box.

"Is this where you get your Kix?" I asked, pulling a box from the shelf.

"This is the aisle," she said, not batting an eye.

I glanced back at Timmy and gave him a thumbs up. I turned back to the woman and asked why she thought people in Britain say "cheerio."

The woman finally looked up and after a moment smiled. "Is he yours?" she asked, nodding toward Timmy.

Oprah was right! The kid really worked. "Why yes," I said proudly. "Isn't he adorable?"

"If you like squirrels," she said, walking away.

Just when I thought I'd found another fruit loop, I turned to see Timmy stuffing Grape Nuts up his nose.

When I met Reba at last week's poker game, I felt a special attraction…

Uncle Al's Swedish Meatballs

- Serves 4–8
- Prep time—about 25 minutes
- Cook time—about 20 minutes

1 ½ pounds ground beef

1 (6 oz.) box of herb stuffing (top of stove kind)

2 eggs

1 small onion (minced)

1 jar (12 oz.) beef or mushroom gravy

1 cup sour cream

1 ¼ cups water

Preheat your oven to 400 degrees. Mix the ground beef, stuffing mix, eggs, onion, and water in a large mixing bowl. Mix well. Next, line two 13 x 9 baking dishes with tin foil. If you don't have 13 x 9 baking dishes, use whatever you do have that can bake meatballs in the oven. Shape meatballs by rolling small amounts of ground beef between the palms of your hands, 1 to 2 inches in diameter, about the size of golf balls. Place in pan and bake for 20 minutes. Meanwhile, mix gravy and sour cream in a large, non-stick saucepan and heat until warm. When meatballs are done, add to gravy and cook on low heat for about 5 minutes. Great for game time or anytime. Simply freeze any leftover meatballs for that next meal.

Clean Slate

When I answered the door on that sunny Saturday in Sidney, South Dakota, I stood face-to-face with a young blonde. She asked if I would sign a card for a chance at a drawing her company was having. I did. She was sexy.

Blondie then reached into the bag she was carrying and pulled out a beautiful set of silverware and said it could be mine free. Before I knew it, she was inside the house unpacking a vacuum cleaner. The deal, I guess, was silverware in exchange for displaying her wares.

"Did you vacuum your rug today?" she asked, kneeling at my feet.

"Yes," I answered, unsure of what I was doing.

"Let's see how good you did." Blondie whistled while she worked. She removed the cleaner filter and proudly displayed the dirt.

I was impressed.

Pleased with my response, Blondie lit a cigarette, sat cross-legged on the floor, and abruptly began to tell me her life story.

"I'm in the process of getting divorced," she said. "My husband treated me like the rug we're sitting on. I left him in Texas and moved up here about a month ago with my two daughters. We live nearby. Alone."

I didn't know what to say. I couldn't help but feel sorry for her as she stared at me through blueberry eyes.

"Where do you sleep?" she asked in a soft southern drawl.

I swallowed hard and pointed toward the bedroom.

"Come with me," she said, pulling the machine behind her. I began to panic. I'd heard about similar situations happening, usually in the larger cities. Sure, I was looking for a companion, but not an instant family.

"You coming?" Blondie called from behind the door.

Like a leery cat, I slunk into the bedroom and clawed at a window to try to open it for some air.

"I need to be turned on," Blondie said as I nearly fell through the glass. Swallowing hard again, I turned to tell her I thought it all seemed kinda sudden.

"Look, I can't..." I stopped short as Blondie stood holding the plug.

"You can't what?"

APPETIZERS

"Uh, uh, I can't believe your husband treated you like a rug," I stuttered. She had me. I felt like a toad without warts. I'd been stripped of all manners decent. She definitely knew what she was doing as she made a clean sweep of my gullibility.

With the contracts signed, Blondie smiled and waved goodbye, leaving me holding the cleaner bags.

If you check out my site on eBay, you'll find a beautiful, seldom used vacuum for sale.

The bags are free.

And before you let a pretty vacuum cleaner saleslady take a bite of your wallet, try these pizza bites. They leave a better taste in your mouth and are a whole lot cheaper.

Bachelor-Style Pizza Bytes

- Serves 4
- Prep time—about 20 minutes
- Cook time—about 15 minutes

1 pound ground beef

1 packet (1.25 oz.) of taco seasoning

1 packet pizza crust mix (6.5 oz.)

1 jar (14 oz.) pizza sauce

1 can (13.25 oz.) sliced mushrooms

Mozzarella cheese

In a frying pan, cook ground beef until no longer pink. With a wooden spoon, break up the ground beef as much as possible while cooking. When meat is cooked, drain the grease and add taco seasoning and mix according to package directions. When mixed, add ½ the jar of the pizza sauce and mushrooms and mix well. Set on back burner and simmer. Preheat oven to 350. Following the directions on the back of the pizza crust packet, mix dough. When the dough is ready, spread on a baking sheet into a thin square layer. Using a sharp knife, cut the dough in half down the middle. Cut the dough in half again sideways so that you have four squares. Fill each center of the square with 2 tablespoons of the meat mixture. Top with cheese. Fold the dough over the top of the filling until the edges meet. With a wet fork, gently press the edges together to seal. Poke a few holes in the top with a toothpick or your fork to allow steam to escape. Bake for 15 minutes, or until the crust is golden brown.

Suckered in Seoul

I began stuffing stuff some years ago. I've stuffed my face; I've stuffed money in my pocket, clothes in boxes, and hay in scarecrows. I've stuffed stuff in the basement and stuff in the trunk of my car. I've even told people to stuff it. But when I stuffed my first mushroom, I had Angie in mind. It's amazing how when you're ticked off you can stuff just about anything.

I met Angie in Seoul, South Korea. I was in the Far East on vacation. Angie was a troubled American with dreams of making it big as a pole dancer singing karaoke to people who had no idea what she sang but marveled at her sliding skills.

And she was successful. Angie was a flowering, climbing vine in a field of nameless weeds.

I went only once to the bar where Angie performed. Well, maybe four times. I can't really remember. But I was there enough to recognize an American female in need of intervention, only because a polka-dotted cat seeks his own.

On the twelfth night at the bar, and on the heels of fourteen shots of rice wine, I joined Angie on the pole as we belted out Elton John's "Tiny Dancer." When the song was over, Angie picked up my shorts and socks from the stage and asked if I was as wild without the wine, John, and a pole.

Kicking my bachelor speak into high gear, I said, "Yes. I'm a cat with spots."

Angie shot me a queer look but invited me back to her apartment. "I don't see many Americans here," she said, locking the door behind us. "What brings you to Seoul?"

"I'm soul searching," I quipped. She wasn't amused. So I tried again. "You have a remarkable pole presence."

"Do you want to get naked?"

"Hold me closer, tiny dancer…" I sang, unbuttoning my shirt. "Lay me down in sheets of linen, you had a busy day today…" I could tell she wasn't impressed with my singing prowess. She was all business as she broke out a bottle of wine and excused herself to the bathroom.

It was midafternoon the following day before I awoke. My head felt like a dried rice cake. Angie was nowhere around. Sitting numbly on the edge of the bed, I tried desperately to recall what happened the night before. The last thing I remembered was trying to slide down the bedpost. I was still clothed, save for my shirt and socks. I wondered if I got lucky. Fumbling for my pants, I noticed that the pockets had been turned inside out. Empty. Angie had her way with me. She left only my plane ticket home.

When a guy flies halfway around the world and still can't find love, there's only one conclusion that can be drawn—I'm cursed.

I'm waiting for the lightning to strike on a sunny day.

If you have ever known someone like Angie up close and personal, try this recipe. The stuffing part is extremely therapeutic.

Stuffed Mushrooms

- Serves 4
- Prep time—about 30 minutes
- Cook time—about 20 minutes

12–18 large white mushrooms

¼ pound pan (ground) sweet sausage or ground beef

½ can condensed cream of mushroom soup (10 ¾ oz.)

Small onion (peeled and chopped)

¼ cup milk

Handful of croutons (crushed)

Butter

Garlic salt

Preheat your oven to about 350 degrees. Wash mushrooms and remove the stems. On a plate or cutting board, dice the stems into tiny pieces and set aside. In a nonstick frying pan, melt a tablespoon of butter; add sausage, onion, and diced stems. Cook over medium heat until sausage is done (no longer pinkish). Make sure the sausage is broken up into small pieces while cooking. In a soup pan, combine mushroom soup and slowly add milk. Heat to nearly boiling, stirring occasionally, and add sausage mix. Stir well. Let simmer about 10 minutes. Next, spray some cooking spray over a cookie sheet. Once sausage mixture has simmered for 10 minutes, remove from heat and begin filling your mushroom caps with the mixture. Fill to the top, packing it lightly. Place each filled cap filling side up on the sheet. Put the croutons in a sandwich bag and crush them to almost powder-like. Sprinkle tops of mushroom caps with crumbs and garlic salt and bake for about 15 minutes, or until the crumbs begin to brown.

Jailhouse Jezebel

I recently answered an ad on a Web site heralding women across America who were incarcerated for "reasons beyond their control" and seeking "pen pals," guys who would understand their situation and write to them.

I bit on the ad like a hungry trout on a fake fly. After all, where better to find an audience to tell a sad life story to than a woman looking for a fool to tell them *their* sad life story?

I eagerly searched the site in an attempt to find the perfect pen pal. It was a virtual fishbowl of barred beauties. I scanned the pictures and profiles and found a particularly interesting photo.

Her name—number 1739810; release date unknown. She was stunning. She looked like she was raised on quarts of wholesome milk, juicy red meat, and an abundance of sunshine that must have stretched from head to natural toe. Her innocuous smile portrayed a beauty who had been unjustly wronged. Her rap sheet read that she had been incarcerated for busting a beer bottle over some dude's head.

I wrote number 1739810, telling her how sorry I was that serving beer had become a punishable offense. She wrote back, telling me what a compassionate man I was and asked if I would write her weekly. "I'm so lonely," she wrote.

"I understand lonely," I replied. Our letters soon became more numerous and intimate. We decided, through our letters, that I would drive to Indiana's Women's State Prison and meet her.

I picked up the jailhouse phone the morning of our first meeting and gently touched the smeared glass that stood between us. She replied in kind. Although the glass was cold and greasy, I felt an instant connection. She was stunning. Number 1739810 leaned close, breathed a breath of hot air on the glass, and drew a heart. Mine melted.

I was quick into my bachelor speak, "Do they allow conjugal sex here?" I whispered into the phone.

"They do, but we have to be married," she answered, brushing her auburn hair from her face. She looked to her left and right. "You know, if you leave me a thousand dollars, I can have one of the guards draw up some legal-looking papers. If you meet me here next week, we can go to one of the trailers for married couples. I know it's a lot of money. And I'll understand if you don't want me." She paused. "Do you want me?"

I dropped the receiver and rifled through my wallet for my ATM card. When I looked up, number 1739810 was pointing to an ATM near a window directly behind me.

"Do you believe in love at first sight?" I asked, drooling into the phone.

"I believe in you, baby," she answered, sensually licking her upper lip.

My hands shook uncontrollably as I withdrew the one thousand dollars. When I finished, I told the guard I wanted to make a deposit.

Number 1739810 carefully counted the stack of twenty-dollar bills and tucked the wad down the front of her shirt. Picking up the phone receiver, she blew me a kiss and whispered, "See you next week... you macho stud."

I did everything in my power to help the following week pass quickly. I got a haircut, bought new underwear, polished my sneakers, helped old ladies cross my street, volunteered at the Y, jogged four miles a day, took tranquilizers, bought a puppy, and wrote a poem for my newfound lady.

When I returned to the prison the following Saturday, I was looking and feeling good. I felt as though I had finally found the true love of my life, despite the fact that she was behind bars. I explained to the old man at the desk in the lobby that I was wishing to see an inmate who was expecting me.

"What's her name?" he asked, opening a big black book that lay before him. I thought for a moment, and then two. I quickly realized I didn't know her name. She had only signed her letters with the letter "Q." Lust had replaced logic. "I... I don't know her name," I said, somewhat embarrassed. "Wait! Wait! I wrote a poem," I said excitedly. "I have her number. Let's see, one, seven, three, she's for me. Nine, eight, ten, she's in the pen. Yes! She is number 1739810. Yes, that's it. 1739810."

"Inmate number 1739810 was released yesterday," the clerk said, closing the book. "Oh yeah. I remember her. Stunning. She left with one of the new guards who quit. Said they were goin' up to Harmony to get hitched."

I stood in stunned disbelief. My psyche once again went into mental meltdown. I had been duped by a pretty face wearing pinstripes. My bachelor itch quickly became a rash. *How pathetic*, I thought. *I couldn't even get a woman behind bars.*

APPETIZERS

As I left Indiana's Women's State Prison, I vowed to shave my head and move to Tibet. That would teach 'em all, I thought. They wouldn't be able to taunt me in Tibet.

I'll send my hellos from the Himalayas.

Himalayan Nachos (Bachelor Style)

- Serves 4–10
- Prep time—about 5 minutes
- Cook time—about 40 seconds

1 box of wheat or rye crackers

1 pound (16 oz.) of yellow cheddar cheese

Olive oil

Hot sauce

Arrange crackers (any amount) in a single layer on a plate. Thinly slice enough cheese to cover all your crackers. Before topping the crackers, break up the cheese into pieces to help it melt faster. Put enough cheese on the crackers to cover the face of it well. Next, take your bottle of olive oil and lightly sprinkle all your crackers (a couple drops on each cracker will do nicely). Do the same with the hot sauce. Microwave 30–40 seconds, or just until the cheese melts.

One Potato, Two Potato

I once worked with Pete Potanski in the potato fields of Pluto, Idaho. It was our job to "debug" nearly eighty acres of potatoes in the northern section of Pluto to ensure that potato bugs didn't chew through the tender leaves of the potato plants.

Check or cash didn't pay Pete and me. Reward for our hard

work was sacks full of the finest potatoes Idaho had to offer. And if being paid with potatoes sounds like the Great Depression, in a sense it was. Pete and I were greatly depressed. We both had lost our paying jobs at a local pickle factory in nearby Pottsfield when we were caught with our fingers in a pickle jar.

In addition to losing our jobs, the women we were dating dumped us for a couple of asparagus farmers from California. All the clothes we owned burned in the fire that erupted when we were shot at chasing the asparagus farmers from California, and Pete had hemorrhoids.

We were penniless and miserable.

The darkest hour in our pathetic lives occurred one Thursday night while siphoning gas from a pickup truck full of potatoes in the parking lot of the Potato City Inn. Pete stood lookout as I crouched near the truck, sucking the open end of a three-foot long piece of garden hose I had snaked into the farmer's gas tank. I had just sucked the gas to the brink of the hose when Pete panicked.

"Someone's coming!" he cried, slapping me on the back, my mouth quickly filling with gasoline. It was the farmer who owned the truck. Spitting gas left and right, I quickly pulled the hose from the tank and stuffed one end down the back of my pants to help hide it, slapped the cover back on the tank, and slid the gas can behind the left rear wheel of the truck. I quickly stood, trying to whistle nonchalantly, but the gasoline burned my mouth so bad I couldn't pucker. So I started picking my nose.

"What are you fellas doin' by my truck?" the old farmer asked as he approached us puffing a fat cigar. I kicked Pete in the shin.

"Oh, uh, we had to stop and pick our noses," Pete answered, shoving a finger up his left nostril.

Pete and I stood looking stupid with our fingers in our noses. "You boys are actin' awful peculiar," the farmer remarked. "What's that gasoline I smell?" he said, poking me in the chest with his walking cane. "You boys stealin' my gas? Get yer finger outta yer nose and answer me, boy!" he demanded, blowing a cloud of cigar

APPETIZERS

smoke in my face. That triggered a chain of events that forever changed the meaning of fried potatoes.

I first gagged on the smoke and then sneezed. When I did, what gasoline was left in my mouth sprayed the farmer's cigar. A huge fire flash caused the farmer to scream like a little girl and drop his burning embers into the tiny puddles of gasoline that had pooled around my feet. That fire flash caused me to scream like a bigger girl, and I turned to run, the hose in my pants following me like a rubber tail. In my angst, I broke wind. I didn't mean to … it just happened. My gas blew through the hose and into the burning gas on the ground. The burning gas on the ground found new fuel and followed it back to its origin, and the seat of my pants lit up like a Roman candle. I screamed again. Pete started kicking me in the butt to try to extinguish the flames, and the farmer was beating Pete with his cane. We were halfway across the parking lot when the tiny fire by the truck ignited the gas can behind the left rear wheel of the vehicle. It was only a matter of moments before the truck exploded. We three stood stunned as chunks of charred potato pieces rained down.

Following our time in jail, Pete and I moved to south Texas and found work on a crab boat. It was there I found the inspiration for this recipe. And, no, it's not a baked potato.

Custom Crab Cakes

- Serves 4
- Prep time—about 1 hour
- Cook time—about 20 minutes

1 pound (2 8 oz. pkgs) imitation crabmeat (lump type)

2 tablespoons of mayonnaise

2 eggs

20 saltine crackers (crushed)

½ small onion (chopped)

½ small green pepper (chopped)

1 tablespoon lemon juice

1 tablespoon Cajun seasoning (optional)

⅓ cup olive oil

Worchester sauce

In a large mixing bowl, add crabmeat, mayo, onion, green pepper, and Cajun seasoning and mix well. In a small bowl, lightly beat both eggs and add to crabmeat. Add lemon juice and 3 shakes of Worcestershire sauce. Mix all together until thoroughly blended. Now you'll need a couple of dinner plates and a whole lot of patience. Here's the tricky part. Very carefully form the crab mixture into medium-sized patties. Let me warn you, this won't be real easy. However, once you get one formed, gently slide it off your hand and onto one of the plates. Repeat this process until all of the mixture is used. Before you attempt to fry your cakes, stick them in the freezer for about 20 minutes or the fridge for 30–40 minutes. The cold will help them hold together better.

When ready, heat your olive oil in a large frying pan and carefully slide as many cakes in the pan as will fit. Fry until golden brown on one side, flip, and do the same on the other side. These are pretty darn good!

COOKING BACHELORSTYLE INDEX

Breakfast

Biscuits and Sausage Gravy..
Egg McBachelor..
Egg Noodle (Bachelor Style)..
Egg and Veggie Scramble ....
Finnish Toast ....
Ham and Eggs ....
Mexican Omelet ....
Portobello Morning..
Restaurant-Style Egg Sandwich ....
Western Breakfast Wrap..

Lunch

Bachelor BBQ..
Barbecued Butter Beans ....
Chicken Pot Pie ....
Hungry Man Taco..
Italian Burgers...
Mabelene's Hot Ham and Cheese ....
Maggie's Club Sandwich ....
Mushroom Steak Sandwich...
Noodle with a Twist ....
Pizza for One ....

Swiss Burger with Mushrooms ....
Taco Beef and Noodle on a Bun..
Taco Salad ....
Tuna Boats..
Tuna and Noodle Express..
The Roast Beef Dunk ....

Dinner

Bachelor's Barbecue Chicken ....
Bachelor Ham and Cabbage ....
Bachelor Roast Chicken..
Bacon-wrapped Chicken on a Bed of Buttered Noodles...........
Barbecue Chicken Bake ....
Barbecued Meatball Sandwich ....
Chicken Quesadilla ....
Chicken/Seafood Pasta...
Dr. Love's Zippy Green Bean Casserole ....
Fried Fish (Fresh or Frozen)...
Glazed Baby Carrots..
Ham and Broccoli Turnover ....
Hamburger Hash..
Lasagna with Beef (not lamb) ....
Lobster and Clam Thanksgiving ....
Meatloaf..
Roy's Winner's Circle Chicken ....
Sausage and Shells ....
Steak and Spaghetti ....
Tater Tot Casserole...
Three Piggy Pork Sandwich...
Zucchini Boats ....

Appetizers

Bachelor-Style Pizza Bytes ....
Chicken Fingers ....
Custom Crab Cakes ....
Fried Oysters ....
Himalayan Nachos (Bachelor Style) ....
Seafood Snackers ....
Stuffed Mushrooms ....
Uncle Al's Swedish Meatballs ....